I was honored to have an opportunity to read
Kelly's book *Leaderfluence*—what a treat!! It
the journey of a humble man who has achiev
of conviction on the essentials of service and ethics in today's world are
reassuring. Those of us connected to Mars Hill University are thankful for
the role his Alma Mater played in his life and greatly appreciate his contributions to the University.

Dan G. Lunsford, Ed.D.
President Emeritus, Mars Hill University

In a field rich with scholarship and advice on how to be an adaptive leader,
one that is capable of leading through the complex and complicated challenges arising in the workplace today, Mike has written an important
prologue. He's addressed a mission-critical starting point, a first step for
leaders who aspire to show up as the best versions of themselves. In *Leaderfluence*, Mike tackles a piece of the leadership puzzle often overlooked
in other books on the subject: How should you lead yourself? How can
you self-assess, calibrate, and improve yourself, such that you will show up
in deliberate, considered ways that allow you to be the person you aspire
to be, while optimizing the impact, performance, and output of the teams
you lead? In *Leaderfluence*, Mike anchors his observations and advice in
candid examples from his own journey, sharing the wisdom gained over a
remarkable career as a senior leader across decades and diverse industries.
The self-awareness, circumspection, and thoughtful approach that Mike articulates here will allow leaders at all stages in their careers to more fully
realize their potential and to maximize their intentional positive influence.

Keith Enright
Chief Privacy Officer
Google

Mike presents a uniquely thoughtful approach to leadership based on his
many professional and life experiences that will empower you with the tools
to lead your organization. This book is filled with great wisdom and practical perspectives on how to achieve a purpose-driven life through leadership
at home, work, and in your community. Perhaps the most poignant advice
is to start by asking yourself if you are leading well through your own mis-

sion statement before you lead others. This is an excellent guidebook for leadership development programs in your workplace!

Kelley J. Downing
Executive Chair
Bartlett Wealth Management

In *Leaderfluence*, Mike Kelly walks you through his journey of personal discovery as a corporate and civic leader, and unselfishly shares what he has experienced and the learning forthcoming. I was moved by the detailed nuances of his conversation. It is obvious that Mike Kelly wants your journey through LIFE to be successful. From him to us...On this Planet, Our Presence Matters!

Clifton L. Taulbert
Author, Who Owns the Ice House?; Eight Habits of the Heart

Leaderfluence is a book that I will return to read again and again. Mike Kelly approaches self-leadership with depth of purpose and earned wisdom. His insights are delivered as an honest, respectful dialogue, and he requires the same from his readers. There is no glossing over the difficult questions of social conditioning, racial inequity, and the hard work of self-reflection. Mike has written a definitive user's guide to valuing ourselves and those we "love, lead, and serve." Beautifully written; I am struck by the depth of the wisdom and the candid and loving way that he writes.

Elizabeth Usovicz
Director
Rotary International
Zones 30 and 31, 2021 - 2023

Over several decades, I've been observing Mike Kelly rigorously develop and consistently demonstrate the concepts he describes in these pages. May we all make bigger impacts in the world as we put into practice the big ideas Mike describes.

Mark Simes
Director of Ministry
Mariemont Community Church

If you're a young person (as I am) wanting a roadmap to becoming a magnetic leader, you must read *Leaderfluence*. Mike Kelly clearly lays out the mindset and motivation anyone must master to be a leader others aspire to emulate and whom they respect. As a dear friend of mine, Mike has made it clear that leadership success doesn't only mean power and prowess; rather, it's a daily act of serving gently, caring powerfully, and loving intentionally. I urge any young person who wants to grow into a leadership role to read *Leaderfluence*.

Hannah Grady Williams
Gen Z | Consultant
OVRTURE Consulting

Through *Leaderfluence*, Mike Kelly expresses his lifelong drive and mission to develop teams by focusing on the development and impact of their leaders. In the desert of modern corporate misdirection, team-oriented leadership is desperately needed. Mike articulates a disciplined path for caring leaders to follow, not to pursue the selfish perfection of the leader, but rather to improve the impact upon and the success of the leader's team. Live a relevant life. Roll up your sleeves and get to work on yourself. Read *Leaderfluence*.

Jonathan Sams
Attorney at Law
Sams Fischer, LLC

What a phenomenal book with steps to success for an individual to lead oneself. Happiness is made within, despite what one faces in the world. Mike's book and experience gives you actionable steps to take before life throws you obstacles you may not foresee. Your attitude and vision help paint your picture of success. Take opportunities, limited or vast, to make your life comfortable. This book is a great tool to succeed with a little sacrifice and investment in improving yourself despite what goes on around you.

Katrina Felder
Lieutenant Colonel
USAF, Retired

Leaderfluence is without a doubt the awakening of where you are as a person in relationship to your leadership skills. Mike Kelly illustrates in a positive way how you as an individual can become the person and the only person who can learn to "lead yourself." This is a must-read for those not yet aware of how or why one should learn to lead oneself to be a positive role model in the leadership of others.

Floyd Lancia
Director
Rotary International
Zones 30 and 31, 2019 - 2021

LEADERFLUENCE

SECRETS OF LEADERSHIP ESSENTIAL
TO EFFECTIVELY LEADING YOURSELF
AND POSITIVELY INFLUENCING OTHERS

MIKE KELLY

HIGHERLIFE
PUBLISHING & MARKETING

Leaderfluence

Published by HigherLife Development Services Inc.
PO Box 623307
Oviedo, Florida 32762
www.ahigherlife.com

ISBN: 978-1-954533-45-5 (Paperback)
978-1-954533-46-2 (ebook)
Library of Congress Control Number: 2021916811

Printed in the United States of America.

10 9 8 7 6 5 4 3 2 1

CONTENTS

———

INTRODUCTION

"He that would govern others,
first should be the master of himself."

–Philip Massinger, English dramatist

ave you thought about what your life will look like toward the end?

As you are reading this book, you still have some time left. Let's focus on the now. Where are you headed? Are you living an intentional life on the path that is right for you? Who has determined that path? The question is—are you leading yourself well?

When we think of leadership, our thoughts often turn to leading other people. We rarely, if ever, think of leading ourselves. What qualifies us to lead in any regard? Many studies have revealed that very few leaders are deemed effective or worthy of their positions. The term "leadership crisis" is often used to describe a prevalent situation in our world today—one in which many leaders are seeking to be served rather than serving the people they have the privilege of leading. If we want to be effective as leaders, perhaps, as Philip Massinger says, we should first focus on leading ourselves.

As a student in exceptional business degree programs and as an executive with incredible organizations such as Michelin, Inc. and Macy's Inc., I rarely had conversations about or received training on the importance of leading myself. While my education and training were excellent, they focused primarily on effectively leading and managing others. There appeared to be an assumption that the most difficult part of leadership was leading others and assisting them in maximizing their potential. There also seemed to be an assumption that leading oneself was relatively easy and that we all should be capable of leading ourselves without help from others. It quickly became clear to me that most of us struggle to lead ourselves well and that this adversely affects our ability to effectively lead others.

In my first job after college, I worked with a colleague at J.P. Stevens & Co. who was an older peer and mentor of sorts. He was so focused on his job that he lost sight of the other important aspects of leadership and life. He worked extremely hard, and was very committed to the organization and the people who reported to him. Unfortunately, he struggled to manage his other priorities and time well. He was devoted to the company, but he did not have the same level of devotion to himself or his family. I watched him burn out—he "hit a wall," which resulted in significant health and relational issues that adversely affected his effectiveness as a leader. He lacked confidence, was unsure of himself, and had difficulty delegating and empowering other people. In some ways, even though I didn't learn everything I could have from this experience, I was fortunate to encounter it early in my career.

This example, along with my own experience of hitting a virtual wall, led to the writing of this book. I have written it for everyone, but especially for those who have not been properly trained, equipped, or encouraged to focus on learning to lead themselves well. I have also written it for members of Generation Z and millennials who are just getting started in their careers. The earlier you can learn the concepts shared here, the more informed you will be. A clear understanding of how to lead yourself well equips you to maximize your life and positively affect those around you. Another benefit is a renewed level of energy and focus, which could ultimately contribute to fulfillment and improved results in the organizations that you own, work for, or serve. There is a strong business case for following the advice of Jim Rohn, a great author and leader, found in this quote:

**Work harder on yourself than you do on your job.
If you work hard on the job, you'll make a living.
If you work hard on yourself, you'll make a fortune.**

The word "fortune" can cause us to pause because when we hear it, we tend to think of money. However, fortune can also be about peace, joy, and satisfaction with a life well lived. We should all strive to live by this insight, and we should also encourage those we love, lead, and serve to do the same.

How should you lead yourself or work on yourself? Start today by gaining clarity on prior conditioning that might be adversely affecting your ability to lead yourself and others effectively. Conditioning often reveals itself in the form of habits that negatively affect a leader's ability to motivate, inspire, and hold others accountable. Assessments and candid feedback are essential to identifying conditioning. This should be followed by the development of a strong goals program, which should include relevant action steps and accountability. Investing in personal and professional development can provide knowledge of self, which is essential to becoming a leader who positively affects the lives of the individuals they lead and serve.

Some of the most difficult work that I have to do begins with me. It has often been easier for me to criticize or blame others for things that went wrong—things for which I held complete responsibility. I have had to realize that it all begins with me. I am the only person I can control. I have heard it said that when you change, the things you look at change. There is a lot of truth to this statement. At this moment, there is an epidemic of blame and refusal to take responsibility in our country. What if each of us looked in the mirror, honestly assessed who we are, and worked to determine the reasons why we are the way we are? What would happen if we then decided to make a very serious effort to change? We could maximize our lives in a more significant way and help others do the same.

Helping others develop and flourish is a very important

piece of the puzzle. The journey is not only about you or me. I have learned that the way I live and lead my life has the potential to affect those around me in either positive or negative ways. I can be a positive force for change or a negative member of society who exhibits behavior that does nothing for the common good. Regardless of your professional position, you are a leader. You are a leader of yourself and others. You are a leader in your family and in your workplace. You are also a leader in the community, and in the areas where you take time for enjoyment and fun. As we work on ourselves and improve in the important areas of life, we gradually become better able to assist others in bringing out the best in themselves.

Have you ever seen a child emulate a parent or an employee adopt the boss's behaviors? If your behavior is positive, the behavior of those around you will probably be positive as well. The same is true if it is negative. Again, it begins with you and me. Self-image is a key part of this, and it is something that we will explore. How do you see yourself? How are you presenting yourself on a daily basis?

I have worked with all sorts of people in my career, but one thing has always been clear when I encounter people who refuse to take responsibility or accept constructive feedback and change—the attitudes, morale, and motivation levels surrounding them are poor. Their performance and that of their team's is low or mediocre. Therefore, take time today to look in the mirror and determine where you are. After you acknowledge where that is—good or bad—determine what you can and will do to take yourself to the next level. Decide what you need to do to be the very best version of yourself. You will be glad that you did, and those around you will probably be as well.

CHAPTER 1

DEFINE SUCCESS

———

How do you define success? Have you taken the time to consider this question? If so, congratulations! You are one of the few people who have determined what motivates and inspires them to live the lives they do every day.

In today's culture, success is often thought of as "having something" or reaching a certain level. It is often subconsciously thought of in the context of the five P's referred to by Ron Jenson of Future Achievement International: pleasure, prosperity, power, prestige, and position. Unfortunately, despite attaining these things, one often ends up feeling empty and unfulfilled, sometimes leading to depression. There are also often regrets at the end of a career or life. Is this truly the definition of success? I would say that it is not and that "What is success?" is a question that each person should answer for him- or herself.

There are many reasons that we often do not take the time to properly define "success." One reason is that in our society, we are conditioned at an early age to go to school and get a great education. We are often encouraged to follow academic achievement with finding a secure and high-paying job, buying a home, and buying a nice car or other material things that the world has to offer.

There is often no real consideration of what is important to an individual. Therefore, a person may pursue an education in a field that offers the opportunity for a higher level of compensation, rather than something for which they have a passion.

When our son changed his college major from finance to communications, I immediately thought that the move was unwise and that it would not allow him to maximize his potential. My assumption was that he could make more money and develop a better understanding of economics if he majored in finance. Why did I think this way? Societal conditioning is the answer. It took me a while to refocus and realize that I was reacting based on my personal conditioning. It was his life—he made the decision, was joyful about it, and we were proud of him.

What is conditioning? Conditioning is subtle, and it begins early in life. It is subliminal, and is affected by experiences with, for instance, family, community, school, church, and the workplace. It consists of the way we view the world based on past actions, experiences, and exposure. Habit development is a key component of conditioning. We do what we do and see the world as we do because of what we have experienced or done in the past. Conditioning can also be materially affected by daily media exposure.

Digital-marketing experts estimate that most Americans are exposed to between 4,000 and 10,000 advertisements each day. This advertising is often very effective for the marketers and their organizations. However, we rarely realize the impact that it has on us. Think of a jingle related to your favorite product. You probably would not have any problem singing it. This is an example of conditioning.

Conditioning can lead a person to subconsciously make unwise decisions—for example, purchasing clothing that you do not need with money that you do not have. Conditioning can also lead you to seek or define success in a way that is not in your best interest or not true for you.

Success is achievable if we define it for ourselves, and if we are intentional about aligning our idea of success with our purpose, vision, and mission. However, this is often easier said than done. We rarely consider our purpose, which directly relates to why we are on this earth. Few of us have gone through the process of thinking through a vision, which focuses on what this journey called life is or will have been about at the end. In addition, most of us do not have a personal mission statement, which indicates what we will do to live out our purpose and achieve our vision.

I recently tested this theory during a speaking engagement, which had approximately eighty-five people in attendance. I asked the question, "How many of you have a mission statement?" How many hands would you guess were raised? Only two!

In my opinion, defining success starts with taking ample time for reflection. Complete the exercise of viewing life today as if you were at the end. What would you like to see at the age of 100 when reflecting on the life that you have lived? Try to clearly picture this in your mind. Then begin the process of painting that picture today. This will help align your purpose with your definition of success. After success is clearly defined, you can realize the importance of focusing your time and energy on the true priorities in your life. Your legacy may then become more important than having or doing. Moreover, you may become more focused on serving and helping others.

Relationships with other people take on even more importance when we have a clear understanding of success.

Defining success is a component of working on ourselves. We often work hard at our jobs, and we periodically feel a need to help others grow and change. However, we rarely work on ourselves in a concentrated and focused manner. Defining success can help us begin the process of determining why we do what we do and, ultimately, the impact our efforts have on others and the world.

The process of defining success can be life-changing. It can also be the impetus for living a life of purpose and leaving a meaningful legacy. Defining success is a very important component of the process of developing a strategic plan for life.

Jim Rohn says that success is something that is attracted to you. It is not something that you pursue. Many people pursue success for its own sake; they fail to take into account who they really are and why defining success for themselves matters. I had no true definition of success. It evolved for me over time. I have come to realize that having the right definition can have a huge impact on self-image, and on the way time and energy are invested. We get one chance at life, and it is very important that we are very clear on what it means for us. The earlier we define success for ourselves, the greater the likelihood that life will be filled with more meaning, joy, and peace, and with fewer regrets.

After I defined success for myself, my life changed in some pretty dramatic ways. I became more focused on what matters most to me. For me, success is about becoming all God designed me to be and helping others achieve their potential. To pursue success, I had to pause and become clear on my current state. Moving from oblivious to aware was part of the journey for me. I learned that only I can and should define success for myself. It would be great if I could rely on others to do so, but that would be irresponsible. Many people might be willing to define it for us, but that gets us nowhere. It is a responsibility that each of us must own.

We all have dreams. But in order to make dreams come into reality, it takes an awful lot of determination, dedication, self discipline, and effort.
—JESSE OWENS, PROFESSIONAL ATHLETE

Defining success sets the stage for building a strategic life plan. This step is important because it allows you to focus on the right thing for you. It helps to determine the *why*. It also allows you to set goals in the important areas of life that we will discuss. Afterward, you can develop action steps related to each of those goals. These are the steps that you will take to achieve those goals while living out your mission in an effort to realize your purpose and potential. All of this requires us to slow down and focus, which can be difficult in our instant-gratification and always-on society.

There is nothing inherently wrong with achieving a great deal in life and with other people recognizing your contributions. The challenges present themselves when we think that it is all about us, and we begin to do things that may lead us to become self-absorbed. I am a person who genuinely enjoys serving others, and I find joy in seeing others achieve their goals. Paul Meyer, the founder of Leadership Management International, describes success as follows:

Success is the progressive realization of predetermined, worthwhile, personal goals.

This definition offers a good description of what we should all seek. We should set goals based on a vision of what we would like to see, and then begin taking action on those goals. As we do so, we can find excitement in the journey, and uncover ways to make a difference in the world and the lives of others. Success is achievable by anyone willing to make a sacrifice and take the appropriate steps.

If you have not taken the time to define success, begin today. By doing so, you will be able to look back at the end of your life and have a sense of satisfaction about the results. You can minimize regrets by taking responsibility now for your own life. Success is not easy to achieve—there is certainly a price to pay. When you set meaningful goals, they do not just happen. Success requires action and a lot of work. The wonderful thing is that you can experience meaningful growth while on the journey.

I was not a goal-setter at one point in my life. My life was all about activity, without a clear understanding of where I was going. In other words, I was working hard at the office to get the job done. My primary goals were the goals that the organization set. I felt that if I accomplished those, I would be recognized and considered a success as far as the organization was concerned. I was missing the most important point: I needed to do the same thing in my own life. My life had become about work, which had begun to shape my definition of success. It is easy to get to the point where a person's identity is tied to their job. However, there are many more important things in this world than work. The worst thing we can do is become a success at work and a failure at home and in other areas of life. If you have not already done so, take the initiative to define success for yourself. It can be life-changing and serve to direct your path toward achieving true and authentic success.

CHAPTER 2

ASSESS THE CURRENT STATE

———

We are often oblivious to who we really are and why. Taking the time to assess these aspects of our lives can be important for our effectiveness in life and the many roles that we play. It can also be critical for living a maximized and full life. Many times we, and most of the people around us, are operating on autopilot. We live in a very busy society. Things are hectic and we face many demands. The effort it takes to juggle those demands on a daily basis can distract us from reflecting on our situation, obtaining adequate feedback, and subsequently making changes.

I was very busy early in my career, and I continually aimed to achieve a high level of success by excelling and looking forward to the next thing. Rarely did I take the time to assess my current state. It was not until I experienced a period where things were not working the way I thought they should that I took the time to stop and reflect on where I was and why. When I did so, I had a revelation and something with which to work. Afterward, as I changed, I noticed that things in my life also began to change.

The reason we do not often assess our attitude and behavior is conditioning. We develop a way of seeing the world that is often difficult to recognize or change. We will discuss this topic in the next chapter. Taking the time to assess our current state and reflect on conditioning can be exactly what we need as we work to take a more strategic approach to life.

Most of us begin the day looking in the mirror. Are we excited about what we see? Some days I am and some days I am not. There is work that needs to be done to get the day started and ended well. The great thing about this is that it causes us to consider where and who we are. We also have the opportunity to think about how we will live and lead each day. That is also true as we consider where we are relative to where we want to be. It begins with looking in a "mirror" and assessing the current state. Who am I? What have I accomplished thus far in my life? What has caused me to excel or miss the mark? What is hindering my progress? When you have clear answers to these questions, consider what you will do about your situation. This is something that will take careful thought and planning as well as introspection and transparency. It may also require input from others or the use of assessment-related tools. If you are seeking a few ideas, here are some questions that you may consider asking yourself and others.

1. What are my strengths and strong points?
2. What are my weaknesses and areas of opportunity?
3. What else would you like for me to know?

These three questions can be helpful as you seek to assess your current state and obtain feedback. I often ask these questions, among others, when gathering feedback while assessing my own performance. Also, I recently incorporated these questions into my work with clients. When I work with someone, I ask them to meet with their superiors, subordinate(s), and peer(s) and ask these questions. This helps them become comfortable with asking for feedback, and helps others become more comfortable with providing candid feedback. Growth occurs on both sides.

A COO of a large international medical company once told me that the higher he had gone in his organization, the more people told him what they thought that he wanted to hear rather than what he really needed to hear. He was a humble and authentic leader, but because of his role, people were intimidated and reluctant to be candid with him. He truly wanted to be self-aware about how he came across to other people, but it was difficult for him to determine this clearly on his own. As a result, he made it a point to facilitate a culture in which people would tell him the truth or what he needed to hear, rather than what they thought he wanted to hear. He became more transparent with his team and shared personal leadership gaps of which he was aware. He was also more intentional about sharing his failures. Ultimately, he began to receive constructive feedback that he found helpful. He graciously accepted the feedback and thanked those who were willing to provide it. Feedback, whether given or received, has the potential to increase leadership effectiveness, results, and job satisfaction.

Another good way to determine your current state is to examine the performance reviews you have received over the years. What do they tell you? Are there any consistent themes worthy of your attention? What were some of the comments about your strengths and contributions? What about your weaknesses? Are there themes that reveal certain tendencies or consistent behavioral patterns? After considering this information, it may be helpful to speak with someone else to get their perspective. It could be the person who provided the feedback or a mentor or coach. The main thing is to begin the conversation and be open to what you hear. It could also be helpful to share what you learn with people outside your work circle. They might have a perspective that is unique and meaningful.

Ideally, you should also request and consider additional feedback that is holistic, such that it comes from beyond the workplace. For example, in addition to your boss and coworkers, you could ask your family, friends, and community or social connections for feedback. This method can allow you to gain a broad understanding of what kind of person you are in all areas of life. Masks often abound at work. Many leaders and those who collaborate with them come to work wearing their "corporate faces," looking to make a difference and impress others. This results in a performance culture in which people act out of fear or in order to quickly advance their careers. On the other hand, if you are at home, you may let down your guard a little more to allow the real, more transparent you to be revealed. Therefore, seeking out feedback from a wide cross-section of people could prove very helpful as you work to develop a better understanding of your current state.

In addition to seeking feedback from others, self-assessment—taking the time to slow down and reflect on our own past behavior—can be useful. Self-assessment can be difficult because it is tough to realistically see and assess ourselves. We have some awareness of our strengths, but often we deny our weaknesses. In order for self-assessment to work, we must be honest with ourselves.

In order to change, it is imperative that we clearly understand our current state. Where are we now, where do we want to go, and why do we want to go there? When the answers to these questions are known, it becomes easier to establish a plan and obtain the help that we need to move forward. Taking time to assess our current state and to make decisions about the future can not only improve our results but also increase our personal satisfaction, joy, and peace.

You may be wondering whether being aware of your current state really matters. It does. Compare it to running a race. If you are running a one-mile race, you need to know how far you have come or the competition may just pass right by you. Knowing the score and where you are in relation to your competition gives you an idea of what you need to do to excel. That is true in sports and in the game of life as well. Where am I and what brought me to this point? After you have clarity on that, you may want to consider what you need to do to move forward. As with any sport, there is a time clock. You have a finite period of time to run your race. You have one life and it will end at some point. Recognizing where you are, and whether you are living a life aligned with your personal mission, purpose, and desires can determine whether you will finish your race with a life well lived. How many people will you have touched along the way? Is this world better now than before? Are the lives of the people whom you have had an opportunity to touch improved? To get there, you must take some time to look in the mirror, see what is there, and respond appropriately to what you see.

CHAPTER 3

RECOGNIZE PAST CONDITIONING

___

Conditioning is a powerful and subliminal force. We are all conditioned beings. Conditioning occurs gradually from the time we are born and continues throughout our lives. Our conditioning can be shaped by past experiences of success or failure. We are subtly shaped by family, community, church, school, and workplace influences, to name a few. Even when we recognize detrimental conditioning or habits, they often prove hard to overcome, especially if we are reluctant to stray away from the tribe or herd. We may not want to disappoint others or break the standard code. Our group can and often does include family, friends, neighbors, co-workers, bosses, or anyone with whom we relate or seek approval.

Conditioning leads us to conform, rather than to break away from the crowd and tread our own paths. For example, corporations spend tremendous amounts on advertising to generate a desire for their products or services. Professional athletes or entertainers are often used to appeal to our interests or alliances. This may lead to a purchase that, if reinforced by a positive compliment from a trusted relative or friend, could lead to additional unnecessary purchases.

In organizations, conditioning can result in a fear of failure, which often leads to a lack of innovation and creativity. Many bright and intelligent people "paint within the lines" on a daily basis for fear of upsetting the boss and losing favor. This could mean losing out on a potential salary increase or promotion. However, without failure, there is often a lack of growth. In other words:

Success is not final, failure is not fatal.
It is the courage to continue that counts.
—ANONYMOUS

The first step to overcoming conditioning is to identify it. This can be challenging, especially as it can be so hard to get candid feedback. Others in your circle of influence are often unwilling to risk damaging your friendship or relationship by telling you the truth. If you are someone who manages or leads people, it becomes even more of a challenge. People often do not want to put their livelihood at risk, so they cater to maintaining the relationship and their place in the tribe. Unfortunately, there is little to no growth in such situations, and change becomes unlikely. Becoming self-aware and developing a better understanding of your past conditioning could allow you to better help and support those you love, lead, and serve.

SELF-IMAGE

One area in which conditioning can plainly manifest itself is our self-image. A positive self-image has been shown to be one of the keys to success. How do you see yourself and why do you see yourself that way? We all have a self-image. When we are alone, we should consider who we are and the vision we hold of ourselves. If it is a positive vision borne out of truth and a good understanding of self, that is wonderful. If that vision is negative and self-defeating, we have work to do. A poor self-image can show itself in negative ways and lead us down roads that, in many cases, we should not travel. A poor self-image can lead to stress, depression, and, in some cases, suicide, all of which appear to be occurring at an ever-increasing rate.

The way we see ourselves is shaped by the experiences we have had at various points in our lives. People, things, beliefs, and behaviors have a tendency to affect us in ways we do not realize. Imagine, for example, growing up as a person of little means in an underserved community. Because of a lack of exposure and opportunity, this could lead to a limited view of what is possible. You would not know what you do not know.

This mindset could and does lead to many deserving people never achieving their true potential.

This could also show up in the workplace. Consider, for instance, individuals who work for companies that do not value them or treat them as an afterthought. These individuals are rarely afforded opportunities for training, coaching, or feedback. They may also be overlooked when opportunities arise for growth or promotion. People like this often limit their goals and merely do enough to remain employed. If they happen to be in over their heads financially, they tend to grin and bear it without addressing the issue with their direct supervisor or others in authority. This may, in turn, lead to a loss of confidence and a leader who constantly second-guesses him- or herself. These individuals matter and have value but, sadly, they do not believe it. They do not feel motivated, and they fail to realize their true potential and the many possibilities before them. This often manifests itself in ways that lead to problems in other areas of life outside of work. It can, for example, lead to stress and affect relationships with family and friends.

As demonstrated in this example, we begin by believing something. What we believe affects our attitude, which influences our actions and, ultimately, our results. If I am positive and confident, those elements show up in my self-image. If I am the opposite, that is obvious as well. My mindset tends to shape my attitude, and I then begin to behave in ways that are subconsciously aligned with that attitude. I act automatically without thinking. Clearly, it is important that each person cultivate, develop, and maintain a positive self-image.

As an African American person growing up in Cheraw,

South Carolina, I realized that there were many Caucasians who did not feel that African Americans belonged in society. African Americans in my community often did not receive the respect or opportunities that they deserved. We have a history in our country of valuing or devaluing people on the basis of the color of their skin, or what they have or do not have. This often adversely impacts the vision that people have of themselves. For me, it has taken years to develop a stronger self-image because society is culturally constructed in a way that makes it easy for a member of a minority group to think less of him- or herself. You become what you believe. I believe that every person is someone who matters. We must respect each other and find ways to build up each other. That is especially true if you are a leader in any capacity. You have the opportunity to build people up or tear them down. My hope is that you will make the choice to do the former.

A positive self-image can be an asset as you work to navigate the minefields in life. We live in a society where judgment has become normal. Do not let this affect you, because you do belong. We all matter. Believe in yourself and surround yourself with positive people. Use quotes, visualization, and affirmations often. They can serve to motivate you and help you stay on track as you move forward. This has certainly been evident in my life. I did not know how I would accomplish many of the things that I have because no one in my family and no one I knew had accomplished them before me. I am referring to things such as going to college, serving as an executive in large corporations, leading at a high level in non-profit organizations, and starting viable businesses. As I reflected on my life,

I realized that my mother, father, and others did a wonderful job of encouraging me in their unique ways. We each have an opportunity to do this for others. When you are tempted to tear someone down with words or actions, think of the potential impact and do the opposite. Think of a way in which you can affirm the person. You never know what impact your words, actions, or inactions will have on that person's self-esteem and, ultimately, the image they have of themselves.

If you see yourself as someone who is a failure, your attitude will be that of failure and your behavior will follow, as will the results. In elementary school, I tried to make the basketball team but was cut. I was devastated and felt like a loser. We did not have the money for me to attend a basketball camp, an opportunity that some of my more financially-abled classmates had. I decided to improvise and turn things around myself. I began to visualize myself as a very good basketball player. I listened to games on the radio. I went to the library and checked out a book on the topic, studied it very closely, and read it cover to cover a few times. I then began to practice the fundamentals I learned, and I played in pickup games as often as I could on the sandlot basketball courts. Lo and behold, the town decided to build an asphalt basketball court not far from my house! That was exciting for me because it allowed me to test what I was learning against older and more seasoned players. Something began to occur as I continued to move toward the vision that I was creating. Over time, I noticed that the older players wanted me on their teams. I also noticed that I was slowly evolving into one of the better players on the court. As a result,

I began to believe that I could be a really good player and that making the school team was a real possibility.

When I tried out for the junior high (JV) basketball team, I made it with no problem whatsoever. The coach developed an interest in me as he observed my commitment, drive, and budding desire. He then spent extra time drilling, coaching, and mentoring me. I ended up as the sixth man on a team that went undefeated! As my self-image became stronger and more positive, I began to transform into a talented basketball player and a more confident person. This positively affected my schoolwork and everything else that I did. I saw myself as a winner and my self-confidence followed. This led to me being a star on the JV team, then captain and most valuable player on the high school team during my junior and senior years.

I ultimately received a scholarship to attend Mars Hill University (MHU) after being recruited by Coach Jack Lytton. I graduated with a degree in business administration. In addition to being named team captain and most valuable player a few times while at MHU, I became the fifth-highest scorer in the team's history during my time there. Ironically, all of this began because I was cut from a basketball team in elementary school.

There are many more examples of where my self-image has worked for or against me. Today, I understand why it is so difficult for people to move from where they are to where they want to be. What you see, you will be. In some cases, this is also true of what others see of you and in you.

**It isn't where you came from.
It's where you're going that counts.**
—ELLA FITZGERALD, JAZZ SINGER

I was fortunate to live in a home where I was loved and my family believed in me. That was also true of the community in which I spent my childhood. Many of the older people there treated me as if I was their child. They were supportive and saw something special in me. That was especially true of my Aunt Dorothy, who encouraged me to persevere and finish college despite the challenges that I faced. Be careful when choosing people to surround yourself with. If they are selfish and lack vision, they will have a tendency to hold you back or discourage you. Develop a vision that is bigger than you can see and grow into it. Let your attitude manifest that vision and your behavior should follow. You will be amazed at the results. The journey, with all its pains and joys, will be worth it. You will also have opportunities to encourage the negative people around you who do not have a vision for themselves. Above all, do not let them distract you. If you cannot positively influence them, do not allow them to restrict your progress.

The day I was offered a basketball scholarship to attend MHU, I went home and told my family, and they were thrilled for me. I assumed that everyone else would be as well, but that was not the case. My friends on the basketball court were surprised. In fact, one commented, "We've seen that team play. You will be right back here with us before you know it." Needless to say, that was not the reaction I had expected. I was expecting encouragement or at least recognition of my accomplishment. After reflecting back on that occasion and other experiences in my life, I realized the role that self-image played and continues to play in my life. I wanted something and felt that I was worthy of it, so I put in the work. In many respects, I was not even clear on the path to take or whether following that path was possible, but I did not let that deter me. I believed in myself and learned to be comfortable with being uncomfortable.

Be willing to be uncomfortable. Be comfortable being uncomfortable. It may get tough, but it's a small price to pay for living a dream.

– PETER MCWILLIAMS, WRITER

The reaction of a few of my friends should not have been that surprising because what I had achieved was not typical for people like us. They had a self-image that was limited; in many ways, we all did. My family did not understand, but they trusted my abilities and felt that I could move beyond self-limiting beliefs and the things that could so easily beset me.

If you have a can-do attitude and are willing to fail, you can accomplish much in this life. Often, your attitude and beliefs will drive your behavior in ways that you cannot see. However, others can see it. Your attitude tends to manifest itself in many ways. It can draw people to you or repel them—that is your choice. A warm, pleasant attitude is contagious. People filled with love, humility, and empathy have always been needed in our world. In my opinion, they are needed now more than ever. The right attitude can result in the achievement of many goals as you collaborate with others.

Think of a manager in an organization who is responsible for several employees. If that manager has a self-image that is positive and appealing, it is much easier to create an environment in which people feel motivated and inspired to do their jobs or to do what is asked.

Think of your own self-image. What is it? How do you see yourself? What is your attitude and how does it drive your behavior? What have been your results? If things are not working out the way that you would like, check your self-image by doing the following:

1. Take time to personally reflect on your values, beliefs, and behaviors. Get a notepad or a journal, and write down your observations.

2. Find a trusted person and ask them for feedback on the aspects of your personality that are most appealing and those that are less pleasing.

3. Find an assessment tool, such as Enneagram or DiSC. Take it, then carefully review and analyze the results.

4. Develop a list of observations based on what you have learned noting characteristics that are considered strengths and those deemed weaknesses.

5. Another important step is to set some goals in the areas where you would like to strengthen your self-image and grow. These goals should be SMART: specific,

measurable, actionable, realistic, and time-bound (discussed more in Chapter 6).

Adopt a growth-oriented mindset. Filter what you hear and keep your life experiences in perspective. Your self-image is what it is currently, but the potential to change is there and can be realized. Be aware of your daily self-image and self-talk, both good and bad, as they can serve to motivate or demotivate. This is something that we can control, but we must slow down enough to realize that it is within our control.

Having accountability in life can often help with self-awareness and taking action necessary to achieve goals. It takes courage to allow someone to hold you accountable. However, if you do, it will pay dividends in the short and long term. Remember, others can often see things about us that we ourselves cannot see. Nevertheless, you are the only one responsible for who and what you become. It is no one else's responsibility. It is a matter of choice. You have been created for greatness, and it is important that you believe this above all else. Know that you have the ability to affect the world in profound ways. The key is to have a positive self-image and a belief in yourself no matter what other people say, think, or do.

Self-image is a factor that contributes to how much of our potential we will use. Have you ever known someone who was talented and appeared to have tremendous potential, but never realized that potential? Why do you think that happened? In many cases, it started in the mind. The person may have been told that they could not achieve their goal(s). They may have lost confidence because the people around them were struggling to achieve their potential. Perhaps the person failed to decide that they wanted to do and become more. There may have been a lack of motivation. All of us face barriers, questions, and doubts at some point. The people who get beyond this are those who have a vision, strong beliefs, and resilience, and who take action. Suddenly, their self-image begins to follow. This becomes more apparent when they experience a measure of success.

For me, an example of this is public speaking. I have had many opportunities during my life and career to speak in public. As a young child, I was asked by the pastor to read the Bible on our church radio program. In college, I spoke in class on topics related to business issues. Then, as a young executive at Michelin, I was promoted to a job that required me to train managers on human resources policies. Many of the managers were at a higher level and more advanced in age than I was. I spent considerable time preparing for those training sessions. However, when I began the initial session as a presenter, I immediately realized that I was not confident and did not see myself as a strong speaker. I became nervous and I am sure it showed. I finished the session and received pretty good feedback. Nevertheless, I realized that I needed to work on my public-speaking skills. As a result, I learned about and signed up for a presentation-skills boot camp that was facilitated by a wonderful executive named Bill, a retired military leader who worked at the company. He mentored, coached, and guided me through and beyond the course. His class was grueling, but it, along with his mentorship and support, led to a dramatic improvement in my presentation and public-speaking skills. I gained confidence and began to see myself as a person who had the potential to be a great speaker. I continued to perfect my skills by reading everything I could about the topic, and I began intentionally seeking opportunities to speak. I even joined Toastmasters International. Today, I am afforded many opportunities to share messages with audiences on a regular basis. That period with Bill helped me become much more comfortable speaking in public. I am now able to organize my thoughts and words, and present them in memorable ways. Audiences regularly compliment me on my delivery and presentations. Public speaking has become something I enjoy, and I embrace public-speaking opportunities when they arise.

No matter how you see yourself today, that self-image can be changed and improved. You have the ability to significantly affect those around you, but remember that it starts with you. How do you see yourself today? Do you have a positive self-image? If not, what do you need to do to change it? Think it through and modify or adjust if needed. Take initiative, as the world needs your gifts.

SOCIAL AND CULTURAL CONDITIONING

We are all conditioned. Conditioning takes place from the time we are born and occurs throughout our lives. It leads to habits that contribute greatly to our behavior. Some of the verbal cues that you heard as a child also shape your mindset. Suppose your parents used the term *no* constantly—"*No*, don't touch the socket" and "*No*, don't go into the street." They had good intentions—they wanted to protect you—but *no* could potentially echo in your mind when you become an adult. You might convince yourself not to take certain risks or steps that might be needed to reach a breakthrough. This particular conditioning could lead you to play it safe and not explore options that could not only prove gratifying but also allow you to make a difference. It could also result in unhealthy fear. Remember, this is all subconscious. We do not even think about it.

Our parents and those who affected us during childhood were navigating their own conditioning at the same time that they were raising us. In most cases, they were not aware that the conditioning existed. They made decisions based on what they had experienced in their own lives and cultures. Their intentions were good, but some of the results—the habits we developed due to that conditioning—may not have been as expected. They did just as we do—the best that they could. As we recognize the impact of conditioning, we have an opportunity to make different decisions, and to recognize and change our behavior so that future generations may have a different experience. This is a great way to think, but it is difficult to execute. We must begin with recognizing our own conditioning.

I had personal experience with conditioning regarding work, which led me to join the "rat race." I was under the impression that, as a man, work was all about "killing it" and "bringing it home." As a young child watching television, I noticed that the man, husband, or dad went off to work each day to earn money to provide for the family, which is what my father did as the primary breadwinner. In my mind, this perception was added to the subliminal messages in the world that encourage us to earn and spend, and to purchase bigger houses, better cars, and nicer clothes, all in an effort to keep up with the Joneses. It was not until I had an awakening relatively early in my career that I realized that this was occurring. I noticed that most of the people around me were also caught up in this cycle of earning and spending, which led to me being caught up in the rat race. Perhaps you are caught up in it too.

What is the *rat race*? Merriam-Webster defines it as follows:

> A **rat race** is the unpleasant life of people who have jobs that require them to work very hard in order to compete with others for money, power, status, etc.

The term is commonly associated with an exhausting, repetitive lifestyle that leaves no time for relaxation or enjoyment.

Yes, the rat race is alive and well. We are stressed, and often find it difficult to take a break for rest and rejuvenation from our jobs, businesses, or other projects. We neglect the people and things that are most important to us, often with little realization that this is occurring. The rat race has a way of destroying individuals, families, and institutions. It can also be the cause of burnout.

At some point, either consciously or subconsciously, we have all been involved in the race. The rat race is subtle. Early on, we are prepared through societal conditioning to strive for more. However, there is a cost associated with this relentless pursuit. We often do not recognize the need for change until a life-altering event occurs, such as the death of someone close to us, an illness, or a job loss. When we come to this realization, it is often very difficult to break ingrained conditioning or habits and make changes.

One of the life-changing experiences I encountered was hitting a virtual wall during my time as an executive with Michelin. That experience led me on the path toward becoming a certified life coach and, ultimately, a certified executive coach. Applying the principles that I learned to my own life has resulted in a tremendous change for the better. I now have a mission to help others realize that they have bought into the rat race and to evaluate the impact that conditioning has on their lives and on those around them. As a professional coach and financial planner, I guide and assist clients and others in developing plans to change and move toward their dreams and the visions of becoming who they really want to be.

Are you in the race? How is it going? Is there a need to change? If so, how will you change? Who will hold you accountable for doing so? These are important questions. They are certainly worth answering—if not for yourself, then certainly for those you love and others around you.

The rat race cannot be won. In general, we should all focus on developing a better understanding of what drives us and consider how the past affects who we are today. What is good about who we are today? What is bad? What needs to change? Investing time in understanding your past conditioning could pay great dividends. It could also be part of the process of determining your current state.

The rat race is just one of the many ways that conditioning manifests itself. However, it tends to have a greater impact on us because work has become so central to life. We spend more time at work than at home. Becoming aware of our conditioning and behavior at work is as important as it is in all the other areas of life. As we become more aware, we can begin to consider what needs to change. A good understanding of our purpose and why we are here can serve as a motivation for changing our behavior and addressing the conditioning that we all have in our lives.

George Floyd's death, a tragedy that—along with the COVID-19 pandemic—turned our country upside down in 2020, reminded me of conditioning. I have been asked to speak to multiple groups on the division and racism that are evident in our country. As I prepare to speak, I am reminded of the impact of conditioning, especially as it relates to race. Bias and unhealthy perspectives on race are a perfect example of conditioning.

I grew up during the Civil Rights Era. If you were Black, you had very few rights. I remember the death of Dr. Martin Luther King Jr. and other leaders during that period of time. These leaders risked their lives to bring about change. I remember integration. In many ways, it was a culture shock for me. In my hometown in South Carolina, Black and White people went to school together after integration. However, if students did not participate in extracurricular activities, there was very little interaction between the races after school hours. Every Friday after school, we went to our own neighborhoods or our own sides of town, and remained there until Monday morning. I also remember seeing a "No Blacks allowed" sign, and hearing stories from those older than me about not being able to use restrooms or drink from certain water fountains. I was told that the fountains were deemed "White only." What a sad time in the history of our country! Think about the conditioning that obviously took place if you grew up during this time and experienced this way of living. Even as a child, it affected me significantly and limited my thinking. I am sure that this was also true for many others during that time. Going away to college and being immersed in a different culture was one thing that helped change my perspective. I had the opportunity to live and study with people from other ethnicities and cultures. I realized that I was important, and that I had gifts and much to offer the world. Nevertheless, it was and is very difficult to break certain types of conditioning. Good or bad, conditioning is something that we have to recognize and make a conscious effort to change. Sometimes, we may need assistance, as conditioning can be challenging to break on our own.

I spoke with a Caucasian businessman who shared with me his conditioning related to race. It was the opposite of my experience, but it was conditioning just the same. He said that he was raised with the understanding that as a privileged White male, he could do and be whatever he wanted. He mentioned that if the members of his family or his friends failed, it was a major event. In his mind, they were set up to succeed and would almost have to plan to fail if it were ever to occur. Over the years, he realized that this was not or is not the case for Black people in this country. He also mentioned that he had an unconsciously biased perspective when it came to Black people. After reflecting and realizing that his conditioning was actually biased, he became intent on overcoming this bias and finding ways to promote healing in our country. In addition to having a conversation with me and other leaders of color, he found ways to volunteer with a goal of making a difference in underserved communities in the city where we both lived. He was intentional about finding ways to break his conditioning. He realized that change cannot happen without effort. When I think about his situation, I reflect on the fact that as a successful business owner, he had people working for him in his organization. I would venture to say that prior to becoming enlightened, his conditioning and unconscious bias affected the way that he led his team, and was probably a consideration when he thought about who deserved a promotion or a raise. This is an example of the impact that racism can have on people in organizations, and they often do not realize that it exists. That is true of the biased person, and for those they lead and serve. We all come to the table with our own conditioning.

Conditioning—unconscious bias in this case—has become an epidemic in our country and it affects people in all segments of society. It starts with us. We have to work really hard on ourselves. We have to expend significant effort and energy on breaking conditioning and growing in order to become better leaders of ourselves and others. What are some ways to do this? Here are a few suggestions.

1. Understand your current state by asking for feedback from others. You can also take readily-available assessments.
2. Slow your pace and take time to reflect on the way that you are presenting yourself, responding, and leading on a daily basis. Live in the present moment. More specifically, value every person you meet and be present during the interactions that you have.

3.   Develop a clear vision of the person that you would like to become.

4.   Set a few goals for changing your behavior. Set the goals in areas that are important to you and based on the feedback that you receive. It is fine to set short-term goals, but you should probably set long-term goals as well.

5.   Commit to taking specific steps for each goal that you establish and write them down.

6.   Find someone to keep you accountable. A coach, mentor, or friend can be very helpful on your journey of change.

7.   Measure and monitor your progress, and do not forget to celebrate the success that I am sure you will experience if you are committed to achieving your goals.

Take this process seriously—it is part of your journey of growth. Change does not happen overnight, nor does it happen effortlessly; it is important that you use a telescope rather than a microscope on this journey, which means be patient and constantly consider the long term. My journey continues, as I seek to grow as a person and achieve my true potential. I constantly remind myself that this is not only important for me, but also for the people I love, lead, and serve—now and in the future. Unconscious bias is one area in which conditioning affects us individually and collectively. Realize and make a serious effort to break conditioning. Doing so can benefit you in ways that you cannot imagine.

We have so much to offer the world. Conditioning along with our view of the world and others can be detrimental to living out our purpose. One of the most important things that we can do is to gain clarity on how our behaviors affect others and ourselves. We need each other, and by recognizing the value of each person, we can alter the culture of division and prejudice in our communities, and change the world for the better. The way we live today is affecting current and future generations in ways we may not intend. Being conscious and others-focused is something that we can all achieve if we make a commitment to get out of our own way.

I did not understand the impact that my previous experiences had on me until I experienced a few challenges as I matured into adulthood. Taking the time to explore this in more depth challenged me to develop a greater vision of what was possible. I gained exposure to and have come to the realization that God created me as He has everyone else, and I have a purpose. My race, gender, economic status, or any of the other labels that society has a tendency to place on an individual does not define my life. As I have gained this understanding, I have developed an increased desire to help others do the same. What about you? Where are you currently? What do you want to do or be? There are many people, young and old, who need to know that they matter and that they do not have to remain who or where they are—regardless of what they know or have been told. The media and the many messages that we receive on a daily basis can guide our thinking in ways of which we are not aware. Taking the time to think and reflect is time well spent. It is a great place to begin, but it does not have to end there. Love, humility, and empathy can help us begin the journey of change, and these very important characteristics can help us to see others as they can be and not merely as who they are today. We can value people as they are and see the good in them regardless of their backgrounds and what they do or do not have. Take time to consider what this means for you; those you love, lead, and serve; and those with whom you interact on a daily basis.

My mother is no longer with us, but this is something that I saw in her. Many people saw our home as a refuge in many respects. She did not judge people. She loved them and sought to encourage them. This was not something that was verbalized, but there was a spirit of love and acceptance. I often observed her as she visited with elderly people, served them, and was there for them at times when their families were not. She did not ask for anything in return. She lived out Rotary International's motto of "Service Above Self." When I was offered an opportunity to join this worldwide organization many years ago, I took it because Rotary aligned with my values and what I saw in my mother's life. Ultimately, my wife joined as well. I have also seen this behavior in others who have had a very positive impact on my life.

My father was and is a servant as well. Not having a formal education did not deter him from making life better for my sister, brothers, and me. He and my mother weathered many challenges, but they continued to move forward. This paved the way for me. You and I have the opportunity to do the same. Self-imposed barriers do not exist in reality. They can only exist in our minds if we allow them to occupy space. Make a decision today to go over or around barriers and, as Gandhi said, "be the change that you want to see in the world."

ATTITUDE

Attitude is a very powerful thing. It affects the way that we think and act. Many of our beliefs emanate from our attitudes. Over the years, I have learned that if I believe strongly enough that I can achieve something and act on it with faith, I often accomplish the goal. By the same token, if I doubt myself, my accomplishments are lessened. Similarly, when I adopt a can-do attitude, I believe that much is possible. I am goal-oriented and excited about taking the appropriate steps to move forward. However, if my attitude is passive and risk-averse, I will have a different response. Our behavior starts in the mind and our attitudes are based on beliefs. If I believe the best and have positive expectations, I will tend to act in a way that models those beliefs. The same is true with regard to doubt.

What is your attitude toward yourself? How did it develop? Are you happy with your current attitude and the results that you are getting in your life, or are you disappointed? The important thing is to realize where you stand and the impact that it is having on you and those around you. It is never too late to modify, shift, and adjust our attitudes and change for the better.

As a young person during the Civil Rights era, I realized the importance of attitude as I watched my parents, Theodore and Lucille, interact with other people in my community and beyond. At that time, they could have been angry and blamed others for some of the challenges that they experienced in life. Instead, my father was principled, committed, and focused on making a difference in our lives and the lives of others. My mother modeled love, and encouraged us to love each other and others. They instilled in us the belief that we could accomplish anything if we had the faith that we could do so and worked hard at it. This led me to believe in myself and to learn from others. It also led me to develop a positive and pleasant personality that drew others to me. It created opportunities for me to assume leadership roles that I never sought or had a desire to attain. As my attitude was positive, positive things began to happen to and around me.

Your attitude toward other people is also important. Do you believe that everyone matters or do you consider yourself better than other people? Whatever you believe will manifest itself in some outward way that can be good or bad. An attitude of superiority repels people. Have you ever been in the presence of someone who has a tendency to put other people down or to compare themselves to others, setting him- or herself in a higher place? If so, I would imagine that you did not feel good about that person. The way that we treat and feel about other people can positively or negatively affect relationships. Leaders have a special challenge when it comes to their ability to motivate and inspire others. No one wants to work with someone who devalues people and places him- or herself above others. This is one reason why so many people in companies all across this world have "quit" but remain on the payroll. Companies lose a great deal of money on a daily basis because of mediocre leaders who have never learned an important lesson—the attitude they bring into work every day and display as they interact with others often shapes the culture of the organizations in which they work. The leader sets the tone. What tone are you setting with the people at work, home, and in your community? Your attitude does not just affect you; it affects the people around you as well. The great thing about attitude is that we can change it. We are not stuck with the attitude we have today. Make the decision to change if you feel the need to do so.

What is your attitude toward the way you live your life on a daily basis? It is important that you not only believe you can improve but also take steps to do so. I find that very few people are goal-setters. We tend to operate based on the most pressing thing that jumps to the top of the list. This results in a great deal of stress and a lack of control, which tend to affect our attitudes. Our attitude toward planning, goal setting, and being disciplined about how we invest our limited amount of time can help enable us to be the very best version of ourselves. When we get things in order, we experience less stress, and less stress results in less pressure. With less pressure, we tend to have a more positive approach to the way that we live our lives. We also have the ability to accomplish more with less effort and to experience more joy. Your attitude toward planning and goal setting can be transformational.

This is an area in which it is often beneficial to seek help, perhaps by hiring a coach, or finding a mentor or accountability partner. My life changed dramatically when I learned to better manage my time and priorities, but developing this understanding was not easy. I had a full-time job and voluntarily assumed a lot of additional responsibilities, such as community service and other obligations, along with taking care of my family. This led to me taking on too much, putting too much unneeded pressure on myself, and neglecting my family. As a result, I experienced a period of stress and pressure that certainly affected my attitude. I was neither believing nor doing my best because I felt that I had a huge load to carry. This affected me in ways that I could never have imagined. Nevertheless, I began to recognize the importance of not just my attitude toward the way I lived my life but also the way I prioritized and managed my time.

Attitude drives behavior and behavior drives results. If you have a positive, can-do attitude, you will have a positive impact on others and often accomplish more than you can imagine. The same is true of a negative attitude. If you doubt, are angry, and often blame others, your results will be affected by that attitude and behavior. I have found myself in situations where I did not like my job and dreaded going to work. Needless to say, I was not very passionate about the work that I did and it showed. My results were not good and neither were my performance reviews. I have seen the same thing in sports. More than once during my time on the high school basketball team, I found myself standing at the foul line with the game in the balance and the ball in my hands. I had not spent enough time practicing free throws and, as a result, I doubted myself. This led to me missing a few key free throws. In one instance, I felt it cost us the game. I did not believe in myself and that came through in my performance. However, it all began with my attitude.

As a leader, I have had similar experiences. Early in my career, I worked in an environment at a textile-manufacturing firm that was somewhat dictatorial and autocratic. The employees were not really respected by many in leadership and, as a result, they were not motivated. They were disengaged and did not feel that they mattered. In this environment, the employees barely did enough to get by. Stepping into my role as a young manager, I modeled the behavior of my peers and superiors and got similar results to theirs, which were unacceptable. On one occasion, I "blew my top" and raised my voice at a direct report in front of others. That was not a smart move, and it resulted in the loss of this employee's trust and respect as well as the trust and respect of the rest of the team. I ultimately realized this and apologized. My attitude had morphed into an attitude of displeasure and negativity, which was not good. I recognized the need to change. I reassessed and shifted my attitude. As a result, I adopted a more participatory and employee-oriented leadership style. My team began to respond to this change immediately because they felt that I cared about them and that they mattered. My attitude was more positive, upbeat, and encouraging, and the people responded to it.

Attitude is not just about us—it also affects those around us. Unfortunately, we often do not realize the impact we have on others. We live in our own heads and see the world through our own eyes. We bring to the table the conditioning that has been underway for many years. Part of that conditioning comes through in our unconscious habits. Unless someone is courageous enough to tell us the truth about ourselves, we just continue to wreak havoc on those that we love, lead, and serve. There is a triangle that I like that has attitude at the top, behavior at the bottom right, and results at the bottom left. It shows that if we transition to a positive flow with respect to our attitudes, our behavior will be positive and the results will be as well. We can gain momentum that keeps flowing. The same is true if we have a bad attitude. We can get stuck in a cycle of bad attitudes, and our behavior and results will reflect it. One great way to break the negativity is to get feedback and then modify and adjust.

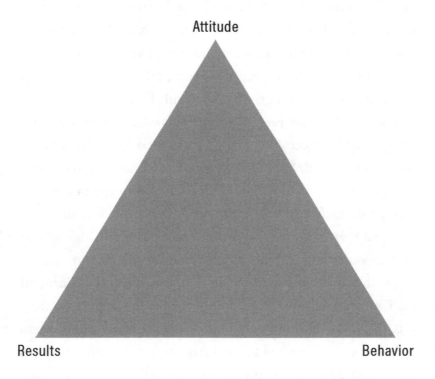

I heard someone say that humility will serve you well if you receive negative feedback. Instead of being resistant to feedback or the person giving it, find whatever truth may be in the message so you can address it and be better as a result. A positive and pleasant attitude can be and often is appreciated in these instances. It can provide a level of comfort and attract others who may be able to help you on your journey of growth. If your attitude is one of love, humility, and empathy, you can accomplish a lot in this world. You will find that people will frequently show up when you need them. Money will often be there when you need it. Resources will arrive just at the right time. The order of your world will be aligned with what is right. However, to get there, we must deal with the conditioning that affects us, often unconsciously.

THE GIFT OF FEEDBACK

Prior to the days of GPS and mobile phones, did you ever leave on a trip with no map and no clear understanding of where you were heading? If so, how did it feel? Traveling without a clear understanding of where you are heading can be extremely stressful and challenging. It helps to have an idea of where we are going. When we get off track—which we all do—it is comforting to get insight and information detailing where we left the track and how to get back on the right path. This example highlights the importance of feedback.

Feedback is a gift that we should all be able to give and receive. It allows us to develop a perspective on how our attitudes and behaviors affect others, because we are often unaware. Our past conditioning leads us to interact and relate to others in ways that are influenced by the habits that we developed in the past. If our behavior is positive and we are affecting people in a positive way, that is wonderful. Unfortunately, that is often not the case. When we are not honoring and respecting others, how do we become aware? Often we cannot because those affected are reluctant to tell us. People tend to tell us what they think we want to hear rather than what we need to hear—the truth. They do so out of fear or a desire to not disappoint. Notably, this may be true of family, friends, co-workers, and others.

It is important to work hard to create an environment where people can and will be honest with us. The primary way to do this is to be authentic, humble, empathetic, and transparent. We must also ask others for feedback and, when they provide it, listen, thank them, and modify or adjust. We need to ask questions to confirm our understanding. However, it is important to avoid refuting what we hear. We should take time for self-reflection after we develop a clear idea of how we are affecting others and then we should set some goals for change. We should enhance our strengths by doing more of the things that are working. When it comes to weaknesses, we should establish goals and develop a plan to move forward by taking intentional actions and seeking help if needed. It is always helpful to have someone who is willing to assist us on the journey, like a relative, a coach, or someone else in our circle who cares about our well-being.

It can be difficult to get feedback from others in the workplace because there is often a fear that telling the truth may result in job loss or other repercussions. Most people are kind and have a strong desire to avoid hurting others. If the person who needs feedback is a manager or supervisor who controls your paycheck and your career, it is even more difficult. I have consulted with and worked in corporations where people would talk to each other if there was an issue with someone, but they would rarely sit down and provide open, honest, and caring feedback to the person who needed to hear it, especially if that person was higher in the hierarchy. This typically resulted in a toxic culture which people "quit" in theory but remained on the payroll. They were not really motivated or engaged, and they did just enough to get by without getting fired. This had a negative impact on productivity and results. The leadership team often sought answers for this in places other than among their own team members. We must make it a point to make people a priority. If people know that they are cared about and valued, they are more likely to be engaged and quick to offer solutions to help the organization solve problems. This, in turn, increases productivity and profitability.

After getting a great deal of experience in various organizations and roles, I once took the opportunity to engage one of my direct managers on the topic of feedback. I had accepted a job with a new organization, and I was somewhat unfamiliar with the role and the industry. After making the move to the company, one of the first orders of business was to meet with my boss and that person's boss separately in an effort to develop strong relationships and establish a good foundation. During these meetings, I had similar, transparent conversations with both managers. I mentioned that I was new to the organization and the industry, and that in order for me (and us) to be successful, I needed honest and candid feedback from them. In addition, I highlighted my desire to provide candid feedback to each of them if the need arose. The conversations were somewhat uncomfortable but necessary for us all. This action ultimately ended up being extremely helpful. I had great working relationships with both of them and grew during my time with the company.

While it was a tremendous organization, it had a legacy culture to some extent as well as a strong hierarchical nature. Employees naturally respected the roles that others held. If they were above you, they were considered "special." For example, I was in the role of a vice president. I remember an employee approaching me and asking if I was one of the "VIPs." I was shocked. I explained my role and I had a great conversation with this employee during which I emphasized that I was a human being just like she was, despite the role that I happened to hold in the organization. This encounter clearly revealed to me that I would have to be intentional about creating an environment in which the team I led and others felt comfortable telling me what I needed to hear rather than what they thought I wanted to hear. I kept this realization in mind going forward. As I led the process of building a new team, we worked hard to create a department in which feedback would be sought, expected, freely given, warmly received, and acted upon. This is something that is certainly easier said than done, but we were strategic and made great progress. I grew from the experience and the team members stated that they did as well.

As a high school and college athlete, I learned that feedback was critical to improving performance. I played basketball for a coach who made it a point to provide positive and constructive feedback. Winning was important to him, but he also wanted each player to be the best person and athlete that he could possibly become. He wanted us to achieve our true potential. As captain of the team, he held me to higher standards and also wanted me to hold my teammates accountable. I did not understand the long-term implications of this at the time, but I do now. The lessons that I learned, such as how to lead and relate to co-workers and create an environment in which others are motivated, have been helpful throughout my life. Regardless of the sport, athletics can provide lessons that are applicable to all areas of life.

Have you ever known someone who was dismissed from a job and had no understanding about why this happened? I have. I witnessed a situation in which someone worked hard, was committed, and thought that they were doing a good job. Unfortunately, that person received very little feedback. In fact, the only time feedback was given was during the annual performance review. When the person realized that they were not performing at the level their manager expected, it was almost too late to change. Ultimately, the person was put on a performance plan and soon they were fired. Each of us has a responsibility to those whom we lead and serve in terms of receiving and providing feedback. If we do this well, we can play a positive role in helping others grow and achieve their true potential. We can also avoid these kinds of situations, which have a tendency to adversely affect morale, relationships, and the culture of organizations.

Another barrier to the flow of feedback is that people simply may not know how to give or receive it. During my time as a salaried employee, I had the opportunity to lead a large training team. At that time, it had become clear to me and many others that the culture in the organization was too "kind" and that candid feedback was not being consistently provided. The primary reasons were that people were afraid of providing feedback and that they did not know how to do so. A small team that included members of my own team, human resources representatives, and operations leaders brainstormed possible solutions to this issue. The team developed an idea for a program called the "Gift of Feedback." The focus of this training program was on viewing feedback as a gift that should be freely given and received. The program included instruction, reflection, and action in the form of role-playing. It was a great way to introduce and soften the topic so that employees at every level could begin to view feedback as helpful.

Traveling without a map or directions is something that none of us wants or should have to do. We should be clear on where we are and where we are going. This is the gift that feedback provides as we travel the journey of life, which includes career and business. To give feedback well, you must have humility and a caring disposition, rather than an attitude characterized by anger, hostility, arrogance, or punishment. If you show up with anger or a mentality of punishment, people may shut down and not be interested in what you have to say. Humility and transparency are powerful leadership characteristics. If you watch and study great leaders, you will quickly recognize that when it comes to their effectiveness, humility is a leadership characteristic that stands out above all others. This is true of many great leaders in the areas of business, faith, government, and community from around the world. Feedback should be candid and authentic. Do so with love and a genuine concern for other people—not to build up your own ego.

Developing a clear understanding of our actions and their repercussions is a lifelong journey that changes over time. The important thing is that there is a mechanism—a systematic way of ensuring that we are receiving the feedback that we need to positively affect the lives of others. We must consider this in the context of our impact on the world during the short period of time that we have on earth. One of my favorite quotes is by poet, biographer, and journalist Carl Sandburg:

"Time is the coin of life. It is the only coin you have, and only you can determine how it will be spent. Be careful lest you let other people spend it for you."

This quote challenges us to consider mission and purpose. As we grow and change, we can better affect the lives of others if we have a genuine concern and desire to help.

In the next chapter, we will reflect on mission and purpose, which are important to consider as we think about the topic of feedback. Understanding your *why* and *how* can motivate you to take the process of giving and seeking feedback more seriously. Most people are good and have an inherent desire to find ways to make the world better. However, in order to do so, we must focus on our own personal and professional growth and development in an effort to reach our true potential.

CHAPTER 4

LIVE ON PURPOSE

———

I n 2018, the average life expectancy for Americans was 78.7 years, based on research from the Organization for Economic Cooperation and Development (OECD). If a person is currently 30 years old, he or she has approximately 17,776 days, or 437,000 hours, before time runs out!

What will you see when you reflect back on your journey and approach the last days of your life? Will it be a picture of someone who made a positive difference in the lives of his or her family and others, or will it be an image of someone who achieved a great deal of notoriety and accumulated material comforts but is approaching the end of the journey with broken relationships, many regrets, and little joy or fulfillment? Each person has a purpose. It is important to stop and consider what that purpose is. It is also imperative that we gain clarity about what we would like to see at the end of our lives. After clearly imagining the picture, the process of consciously painting it should start or continue today. Crystallizing our thinking and developing a strategic life plan may be helpful in this area.

As we all know, each minute, hour, day, and year is precious, despite the fact that it is easy to take time and relationships for granted. To live a full and meaningful life, we should be intentional and take the time to prayerfully consider and visualize the end of life.

The process of "painting the picture" should begin with an understanding of your purpose, vision, and mission. One exercise that you can use to do this is to determine the roles you play in all areas of life and with whom you play them. Then ask yourself what you would like those you love, lead, and serve to say about you at the end of your life. Are you living your life in such a way that these people would say what you desire? If not, do not lose heart or become discouraged. Determine what needs to change and begin the process of intentionally making those changes.

Time passes quickly. In our busy culture, we can become oblivious to this fact. It is nice to occasionally review material, such as the poem written by Linda Ellis titled "The Dash." If you have not read it, I encourage you to take the time to Google it. It will be worth the few minutes that you will invest in finding and reading it. It could prove helpful as you begin the process of visualizing THE END and developing a strategic focus for the remainder of your life.

PURPOSE

Starting with *why* can be life-changing. It can help us to consider purpose in a new way. By starting with *why*, we begin to focus on maximizing the remaining moments, hours, days, weeks, months, and years in ways that matter. It means getting clear on what we want to accomplish in our lives, and it determines what our legacy will be, as each one of us will have one. The challenge then becomes determining how to live that out starting today. Working through this process can serve as a catalyst for evolving toward a purpose that is bigger than we are. Taking the time to develop a vision of what that looks like is challenging, but it provides a certain level of freedom.

Once you do this, it should not be kept secret. The process should be something that you want to share with others and encourage them to undertake as well. Many people live aimless lives, focused on doing just enough to get by. They lack an understanding of or interest in getting clear on their purpose. Whether people, especially leaders, realize it or not, this lack of purpose can negatively affect the individuals with whom they interact. Leading from a place of purpose fosters passion and a strong desire to make a difference in the lives of others and the world. It also helps in recognizing and overcoming the challenges and distractions that impede progress.

For most of my life, I worked without considering my purpose. I accomplished things, but I had no good understanding of my *why*, and I ran into few others who did. In school, it was about getting good grades to get a good job. Getting a good job sounded fine at the time, but as I grew older, I realized that there was so much more. Getting a good job often ends up meaning making a salary and spending it to keep the economic engine going. This can result in stress and debt with little life fulfillment. It means getting on a treadmill that is running at a high speed, which makes it difficult to get off. I had the opportunity to work in the retail industry. While there, I realized that marketing focused primarily on subconsciously influencing consumers to purchase goods. On more than one occasion, I interacted with and mentored young leaders, inside and outside of the company, who were making great salaries but yielded to these types of marketing messages and as a result, carried burdensome debt. These were very talented people with great intentions, but they lacked a *why*. If we started helping young children understand their purpose, they would mature as individuals who are more thoughtful about how they spend their precious time and energy as well as the money earned from their efforts. This would shift the paradigm away from a world in which people trade dollars for hours, live with high levels of stress and anxiety, and have little to show for it at the end of their lives.

My life changed dramatically when I began to better understand my purpose. I realized that I have a passion for serving, equipping, and positively affecting others as they travel their journey in life. We are born selfish human beings, and it is not until we realize that life is not all about us that we begin to experience some of life's richest blessings. I was a busy person, juggling family, career, community, and a number of other things in my life. I was busy with activity, but had no sense of where I was going. At the time, I worked for Michelin, a large, international manufacturing firm. I loved the work and enjoyed the people with whom I worked. We were growing as an organization, and I excelled and continued to receive opportunities to do work that challenged and inspired. Most of my days were spent at work—ten to twelve hours. Over a period of about two years in the early 1990s, I gained thirty pounds and started to have health problems. Nevertheless, I continued to work and stretch myself. It was not until I started to experience pounding headaches and an inability to sleep at night that I realized I needed to see a doctor, who prescribed medication to help with headaches and sleep. I purchased the medication and took it. However, I didn't experience any relief from the pain. Still, I continued to work hard and for long hours. Ultimately, I realized a pressing need to see the doctor again. After a few more visits, the doctor suggested a CAT scan of my head. He scheduled an appointment, and I went for the procedure. I returned to the doctor a few weeks later for the results, and was told that the scan was clean and no physical medical issues had been identified. However, he suggested that I needed to address my mental health. In his professional opinion, I was probably under severe stress and headed for depression. I was shocked! I was a relatively young and healthy former college athlete. I did not think that what he was saying was possible. However, I realized that I needed to change after getting additional input from my wife, who shared with me that my life was out of balance and there was a need to change. She also agreed to support me. This led me on a journey that resulted in significant life change. I ultimately became a life coach. I also gained a better understanding of my purpose and conditioning as part of that process. I took on the challenge to slow down and consider my life journey in a more intentional way.

I am a true believer in the importance of using a "telescope rather than a microscope" as we live our lives. Time passes quickly, and we have very little to waste. Being intentional, aware, and focused are very important. It is also important to understand the big question, which is "Why?" Why am I here? What can be accomplished through me?

To gain clarity on *why,* ask yourself a few questions, such as:

1. What are my gifts?
2. What am I passionate about?
3. What are some of the needs that I have identified in the world?
4. What contributions would I like to make to the world during my short time here?
5. What roles do I play and with whom do I play them?

These are just a few questions—there are many others. In many respects, a big part of the reason we are here is to serve God and others. That important fact can be lost as we strive to achieve and accomplish without a clear understanding of why we are doing so. There are things that are much more important than what I do, what I have, or how people view me. I have come to understand that the relationships that we develop and the people that we help will live on long after we are gone.

What is your purpose and how are you living it out? If you are not clear on this, please seek help. There are many things that you can spend your time considering, but gaining clarity about your purpose is one of the most important things that you can do. Purpose is not something limited to the most privileged in our society. It is something that we all have. Do not judge or limit your thinking based on what you do or do not have. Becoming clear on your purpose can help motivate you to step beyond what has been and move toward what can be. Once you are clear, there is a good possibility that you will be motivated to exceed what you thought was possible. What others have done or are doing does not matter—it becomes more about you and your potential. If you do not believe that this is true, make the decision and give it a try. Associate with people who believe in you. Seek clarity in this area of your life. When you have that clarity, find a way to help others identify their purpose. My purpose is to help my family and others become all that they are designed to be. I have realized that at the end of my life I would like to reflect back and know that I have invested my limited time on earth in a way that has made life better for others. What will that view be for you?

VISION

What you envision, you will become. I remember having a desire to work for an international company and to work for a publicly-traded company at the senior-leader level. I wasn't sure how I would do it, but I had a vision of doing so. At the time, I did not personally know any Black leaders who had achieved my desires. I had only seen them in *Black Enterprise* and *Jet* magazines. From the images and information I saw, I developed these visions, through reflection, introspection, and input from others. As I started to progress toward these opportunities, I realized that it was important to adopt a strategic perspective when thinking about and visualizing life. When strategy is discussed, it is normally in the context of an organization or business. I have come to the realization that strategy may be even more important in life than it is merely in business. A strategic approach to life allows us to avoid wasting a lot of time on things that do not align with our purpose and desires. Without this compass, life can take us on a journey that we may not necessarily desire.

Purpose and vision are parts of our journey. We were each created for a purpose that will become clear to us if we slow down long enough to contemplate it. You are special and the world needs you to shine. You have gifts that you should not hide or take to your grave. The motivation to share those gifts can come when you develop a good understanding of this fact and develop a vision that is bigger than you can currently imagine. Sometimes our circumstances limit our ability to think beyond what we can see.

As a young person, I found reading as one way to increase my perspective and to gain exposure to things beyond what I could see. My mother encouraged me to read, which inspired a thirst for knowledge. As I read, I gained exposure to a world that was beyond my small hometown and what I could see at the time. My parents and many of my ancestors had limited opportunities, which is something that I did not understand as a young person. The world presented barriers that made it extremely difficult for them to move forward without trials and challenges. Unfortunately, the culture of race in the United States is built around a structure that is inhibiting and can theoretically hold one back mentally, socially, and economically. As I read, I began to understand that there was more. The more I read, the more I wanted to read and understand. Regardless of where a person is today, so much more is possible.

As a young person having graduated from college and entering the business world, I saw very few people of color in higher-level management and supervisory roles. Throughout the course of my career, I have never reported to a leader who looked like me. Most of my managers were Caucasian males, with a few Caucasian females sprinkled in along the way. Developing a picture of what was possible, despite barriers that were seen and unseen, was not easy. Nevertheless, the opportunity to attend Mars Hill University exposed me to possibility thinking and led me to open my mind to potentialities despite what I had previously seen. I started down the right path and, ultimately, began to achieve success and accomplish meaningful goals. This confirmed my belief that more was possible. It also helped me find opportunities to lead people from all walks of life and to serve as the model I did not have in my career. In many respects, it gave me and others hope and a roadmap. This led to many fulfilling relationships as I mentored and encouraged others.

Most of us know what we need to do, but it is often helpful to have someone ask us the difficult questions, which can lead to visions being created, enlarged, and realized. When we grow, we have a responsibility to help a variety of others grow and not center our efforts only on people with whom we are comfortable. We must become an ally to marginalized groups and help them with the hope that they too will help others. Although there were no African-American leaders at higher levels on my journey, there were Caucasians who took an interest in me, and I am thankful that they did. My performance, character, and contributions were recognized, which led to a designation of high-potential leader. The training and additional exposure that I received as a result served to increase my confidence, and I experienced significant personal and professional growth. So much is possible if a person is able to see beyond their current circumstances and develop a bigger vision than they currently have.

How do you develop a strong vision for your life? A few steps you can follow are:

1. Pause, reflect, and envision your desired future. What do you see?
2. Consider what you are passionate about and what interests you. What would you want to do even if you were not receiving a paycheck? What gives you joy?
3. What are your gifts? What are the areas in which you have excelled and have received accolades?
4. What needs in the world would you like to see solved and feel that you are well equipped to address?
5. Looking back from the end of your life, what would you like to see, have done, or become, and why?

These are just a few questions to get you started. Do not become frustrated if it takes time—that is expected. Do not rush the process. Instead, give yourself grace. How can you use your gifts to serve others so that at the end of your time you have made a difference in their lives? Gaining clarity as you continue on this journey will bring a sense of freedom. It will relieve the pressure of striving to achieve something that others have in mind for you. Be certain of your purpose and have a clear vision of what living it out looks like. This can bring you a measure of peace that surpasses all understanding. It can also lead to joy on the journey and a sense of fulfillment.

It is crucial to think big and not limit yourself or allow others to be a barrier. Be innovative and creative as you go through this process. As you do so, you will be exposed to new thoughts, information, and insights. Leaders who have done great things are often people who—for whatever reason—thought bigger than anything they could ever have imagined with their natural minds. Each person has the same opportunity, regardless of where they have come from or what they have, and regardless of their color, nationality, gender, or anything else. The only real limits are the ones that you place on yourself. After you clarify your purpose and develop a big vision, you will be ready to determine your mission, which encompasses taking the steps necessary to realize your vision.

MISSION

Living a focused and inspired life begins with developing a relevant personal mission statement and effectively investing and managing your time. A person with a clear and compelling mission statement that is aligned with a clear purpose (the *why*) and vision (the *what*) of the future is quite rare in our world. Thoughtfully considering and going through the process of developing a personal mission statement is undoubtedly worth the investment of time. Throughout my life and career, I have found that rarely will anyone encourage this type of introspection. The reality is that we should not rely on others. Developing a clear and compelling mission statement is something for which each of us should take full responsibility.

Living without consciously understanding how we want to live can lead to an aimless existence. That is one great thing about a mission statement—it can serve as a compass as we navigate the terrain of life. It provides clarity and can assist us in making decisions related to how we will invest our precious time and resources. It also makes it easier to know when and to what to say "yes" or "no." Saying *no* can be very difficult for many of us. That is especially true if we want to avoid disappointing others. I have heard it said that the word *no* is more difficult for people to say than it is for people to hear. Someone making a request has probably been told *no* on so many occasions that he or she expects to hear and often welcomes the word. After hearing this, I reflected on my experience as a salesman. I actually became immune to hearing the word *no,* and I began to assume it meant *not yet.*

After developing my own mission statement, I found that I was more focused and motivated to grow and strengthen my skills. In many ways, going through the process of developing a statement made me a much stronger leader. My mission statement is as follows:

To use my leadership and financial skills to help my family and others grow to become all God created them to be while continuing to grow myself.

I developed the statement around 2004 after having a few traumatic experiences in my life, like losing my mother. She was one person who was very instrumental in helping me become the person that I am today. I would assume that she knew her purpose and had developed a mission for her life because she certainly left a legacy of love, humility, and service that still resonates with me today.

My mission statement helped me make a few major decisions in my life. One was to leave my long-term employer, Michelin, to transition to a new employer, Macy's, where I was offered an opportunity to work in a learning and development role that was not clearly defined. As I considered the opportunity over a lengthy period of time, I ultimately made my decision and took the risk of leaving an organization that I respected (and respect to this day) to take the new role. The deciding factor was the fact that the role at Macy's aligned with my personal mission statement, which is all about helping others to grow.

After making the decision and moving to the new organization, there were some days that I questioned why I made the decision. When those times came, it was always helpful to remind myself of my mission. That thought process kept me focused, and allowed me to overcome negativity or any barriers that I faced. I found it interesting and challenging in some ways to move from an international manufacturer to a Fortune 500 retailer located primarily in the United States. Nevertheless, the opportunity appeared to be just what I needed at the time. I persevered and had the opportunity to sell a vision of creating a new function and department within a division of

Macy's. I ultimately got approval, and I commenced building a team and department that supported the learning needs of the entire division. The department consisted of an instructional design team, an e-learning team, an analytics team, a facilitation team, and a leadership-development team. I was blessed to work with a very talented group of people who had a focus similar to my own.

In my current businesses, I am fortunate to have the opportunity to speak frequently to groups. I often ask audiences: "How many of you have a mission statement?" I have consistently seen that only a small percentage—3 percent or less—have a personal mission statement. When I ask audiences whether their organizations have a mission statement, as I often do before asking if audience members have individual mission statements, the answer is unequivocally yes. People are often excited about sharing their organizations' mission statements. However, when I inquire about their individual statements, their excitement wanes, and I find a look of wonder on the faces of those in attendance. Why does this dichotomy exist? We are often easily led, and we are wired to follow someone else's mission and not establish our own. Creating a mission statement helps a person lead well from a place deep within their soul. It can also make life more meaningful.

Based on my experience, I would surmise that a small percentage of people have a written mission statement. A slightly larger percentage have thought about it but have nothing written down. The rest have not even considered a mission statement.

How is a mission statement created? Begin by considering

the various roles that you have assumed. Every person has a multitude of responsibilities and roles that he or she plays in life. These roles could be, for example, spouse, daughter, son, father, mother, brother, sister, employee, or boss. They are often assumed with little regard for their importance or their impact on others. It is easy to float through the day thinking of pressing priorities and needs without regard for the many important relationships and people in our lives. It is important to intentionally take the time to evaluate the roles that we play while understanding that our roles are not our mission or our purpose. After this step has been taken, we should consider with whom we have the respective relationships.

When we gain clarity about roles that we play and with whom, we should consider what we would want people we have impacted to say about us in the future or at the end of our lives. This is how you take a strategic approach to life. For example, think about your spouse, children, friends, or acquaintances. What would you want them to say about you? Is it that you listened to, spent time with, and loved them? If so, what are you doing on a daily basis to ensure that this occurs?

Mission statements are important, but they can sometimes be difficult to develop. However, the time invested in their development could pay dividends that will last for generations. In the process of creating a mission statement, there are several things to keep in mind:

- Be patient,
- Think holistically,
- Make it personal,

- Determine your dreams,
- Reflect on your values and motivations,
- Journal or document your thoughts,
- Incorporate your faith, and
- Be transparent and honest with yourself.

Successfully developing a meaningful mission statement and intentionally living by it will lead you on a path toward a measure of true and authentic success. It will serve as a foundation for establishing short- and long-term goals in the most important areas of life. A compelling mission inspires you to live out your purpose and the vision that is derived from your purpose. You are here to positively affect the world and make a difference in the lives of those around you.

Creating and integrating an empowering personal mission statement is one of the most important investments we can make.
—STEPHEN COVEY,
EDUCATOR, AUTHOR, ENTREPRENEUR

CHAPTER 5

CLARIFY ESSENTIAL LIFE PRIORITIES

━━━━━

W hat do you think of when you hear the words "life's priorities"? There are a multitude of priorities in our lives and many of them we rarely consciously think about. We operate day-to-day with the intention of taking ownership of responsibilities, doing what is right, and living good lives. However, in our society, it can be difficult to find the time to consider how we are actually investing our precious time. A lack of awareness in this area may lead to frustration and lack of satisfaction. We can accomplish many things, but very few of them may align with our purpose and mission. Neverthe-

73

less, those around us may consider us successful based on their personal definition of success, which is most likely centered, at least to some extent, on pleasure, prosperity, power, prestige, and position.

As we think about our purpose and the mission in life, we must also consider how we can best live them out. Is there a prescription that we can follow that will make things better? Unfortunately, most of our models are somewhat flawed. The people we observe and emulate are typically chasing something, but they, too, may not have clarity about what that is. Many use their time and energy to maintain the status quo. I have heard it said—and you probably have as well—that people never regret not having spent more time at the office. Their regrets are often around other things that they did not do or relationships they did not value when they had the opportunity. This is where evaluating, clarifying, and understanding our true priorities may be helpful.

In life, we are constantly forced to make decisions regarding our priorities. Some priorities may be spiritual development, family relationships, health and wellness, earning money, and more. It is important to gain clarity on what your true and most meaningful priorities are. One way to do so is to reflect back on your purpose in life. Carefully review and think about your priorities, then determine what areas of your life require more focus and attention. Once this is done, determine how you are doing in those areas, and then prioritize them from most important to least important. When you identify gaps, it is important to determine what you will do to fill them.

There are many descriptions of life priorities and types of

wheels of life. I tend to like the "Seven Fs" of Dr. Ron Jensen of Future Achievement International: faith, family, fitness, finances, fun, firm, and friends. These are relatively easy to remember, which makes the wheel easy to apply and share. Future Achievement International focuses on helping individuals and organizations improve their results and achieve their potential. Leadership Management International, which has a similar focus, offers another model: family/home, financial/career, mental/educational, physical/health, social/cultural, and spiritual/ethical. These may take a little more time to recall, but they work as well and a variation of them will be used here.

SPIRITUAL AND ETHICAL

The spiritual and ethical component of life is the most important to me. We have all been created for a unique purpose. What is your purpose for living? Who or what do you represent? In our world, it is so easy to become complacent and feel that we will be here forever. That is especially true when we are young, with much energy and potential. We can tend to make assumptions and take things for granted. The spiritual and ethical component of life could make all of life better if we developed a good understanding of what this means for us, especially at an early age. What principles do we live by? Why do our lives matter? Many people are searching for answers. They are tired of chasing dreams and aspirations and attempting to "keep up with the Joneses." Money has a way of taking a central place in our lives. Our capitalist society can lead us to take shortcuts and live lives that are unethical and selfish. We can develop a tendency to live for today and lose our moral compass just to achieve and earn more. The problem with this way of viewing life is that it is possible to achieve prestige in a job or even be promoted and still feel empty. Suicide has become a near-epidemic today. There are many reasons for this development, including mental health issues. However, some suicides might be related to unmet expectations or getting caught up in the rat race of life, which is virtually impossible to win. As Henry David Thoreau so insightfully suggested, I make myself rich by making my wants few.

I grew up attending a very conservative and charismatic church. My parents modeled what it meant to love unconditionally, but most of the sermons preached at our church were intended to create fear. We were told what not to do, which led to compliance rather than a true change of heart. Fundamentalism had an adverse impact on my faith and the faith of many others who attended. It led to a focus on performance, especially among many of us young people. Much of my spiritual life at that point was about the head rather than the heart. I operated out of compliance. This led to a life of being a "good guy" but not someone who was authentic and living a life of love and joy. It was more about Mike than about other people.

As I grew older, I realized that this was not the right way to live. It took pain, disappointment, and a multitude of mistakes for me to shift my thinking. I have learned the principles that are essential to authentic success, and I now work harder to incorporate them into my life. The world is screaming for people who are genuine and authentic, who follow a set of ethical principles, and who are quick to place others before themselves. We are currently experiencing a level of chaos related to race, economic, and health issues and disparities, which are leading to broken relationships and a great deal of pain. We each have an opportunity to play a role in changing the course of our world and making it a better place. What role are you playing in making this happen? How are you affecting the people you love, lead, and serve as well as others with whom you come into contact?

Living by faith and living with integrity can lead to joy, fulfillment, and peace. It can also influence your decision-making and help you through difficult times. Having a compass and understanding how to make the correct decisions is so important, as is having a filter or means of processing decisions. Surrounding yourself with positive people who are seeking to do what is right is also vital. We tend to become like the people around us. Relationships affect us subconsciously and subliminally. Having the right role models, mentors, and people who are willing to provide accountability is important, as it is so easy to be influenced by others in either positive or negative ways.

When I hear the word *integrity*, I think about the internal. I think of leadership from the inside out. It begins with my mind and my heart. What do I truly believe? Do I believe that I am loved by God, and that people matter and are His creation, or do I have an elevated opinion of myself and feel that I am a god and can use people? Integrity and character are about what we really believe, which influences how we live and treat others. I have seen people who are arrogant and take others for granted. They disrespect and use others for their own purposes, then discard them. This happens in large and small organizations alike. People show up and work hard, but they often do not feel valued at the end of the day. I have also seen and worked with people who were in higher-level positions but willing to serve others lower in the hierarchy. People matter to them, and they willingly model servant leadership. They are people of character who are unselfish, and others tend to gravitate to them. People are often better because their lives crossed paths with these individuals. I would imagine that if you thought back and considered your own life, you could think of both types of leaders, with special memories of those who were authentic and valued you.

The spiritual and ethical component of life deserves serious consideration and reflection. We get only one life, and each decision that we make on a daily basis can affect people now and for generations to come. If we gain clarity on our purpose and live with the end in mind, we tend to lead different types of lives. We often end up valuing people much more than things.

As previously mentioned, I am a member of a service organization called Rotary International that has the motto "Service Above Self." Our members are people from all faiths, ethnicities, and walks of life. The theme that brings us together is service and a motto called "The Four-Way Test." The test asks the following:

Is it the truth?
Is it fair to all concerned?
Will it build goodwill and better friendships?
Will it be beneficial to all concerned?

These points align with the way I see the world. They are also the cornerstones of how I strive to live my life. I often do this imperfectly, but I have the right intentions. I have learned that life is much more meaningful when I operate with an "others" focus. No one lives in this world alone—the sooner we learn the importance of valuing others, the better off we will be. Most of us tend to favor people with whom we are comfortable. We tend to subconsciously devalue people who do not meet our standards. This is one thing that has fueled the divisions we currently see in our country. Racism and hate are inconsistent with the message of the gospel, which is love. Slow down and understand the role that the spiritual and ethical component of life plays in reaching our true potential. This can lead to meaningful change and allow us to live fuller lives. When we live in a box, it can be difficult to realize what we are missing. The growth that can come from stretching and connecting with different people can be freeing, and it can allow each of us to maximize our potential and make greater contributions to the world.

I rate the spiritual and ethical priority of life high and I strive to integrate it into all the other areas of life. Where do they fit for you and why?

This aspect of life, which informs all others, is worthy of much more attention than I can give it here. If we live only for what we see, our perspective and existence may be severely limited. We would also likely miss out on much of life. The fact is that each of us will die. The topic is something that we may not be comfortable talking about very much, but as we mature and increase in our faith, doing so becomes easier. When we become comfortable with this fact and have a good understanding of what it means, we can then begin to really live. We may become more intentional about how we treat others, how we allocate our finances, and how we invest our time. This can leave us free to ethically innovate, create, and work to affect the lives of the people we love, lead, and serve in the areas where we live, work, and play. We can become a positive example, an inspiration, and an encouragement to others. We may also find we are able to live our lives with fewer regrets.

I was recently with a friend, Jonathan, and we discussed the importance of living on purpose. He is someone who has accomplished much in his life. During our conversation, he mentioned a song by Steve Green that includes the lyric, "May those who come behind us find us faithful." I consider this a key statement when it comes to legacy. It puts many of the things we experience, think, say, and do into a different perspective. Will those who come behind you find you faithful? How would you answer this question? If you have not thought about it, now is a good time to do so.

Creating a daily routine that allows you to carve out time for reflection can be transformational. It can allow you to reflect on where you have come from and assist you in realizing how blessed you are, rather than taking life for granted. It can also allow you to free your mind of the clutter that so easily confuses us and weighs us down. In addition, it can be a great opportunity to think of all of the things for which to be thankful.

Reading great books can be part of your routine and serve to inspire, inform, and educate. I find inspiration and encouragement from the Bible and many great works that have been written by talented leaders in all segments of society.

The spiritual and ethical component of life is important, and it can be essential to success and fulfillment in the other priority areas of life. If you have not contemplated what it means for you, this is the perfect time to start that process. If you need help, there are many people who would be willing to listen and provide encouragement. The important thing is that you are willing to take the initiative to ask. An investment of time and energy in this area will pay dividends beyond your lifetime.

I'd rather see a sermon than hear one any day; I'd rather one should walk with me than merely tell the way. The eye's a better pupil and more willing than the ear, Fine counsel is confusing, but example's always clear; And the best of all the preachers are the men who live their creeds, For to see good put in action is what everybody needs.

—EDGAR GUEST, POET

FAMILY AND HOME

Family and other important relationships is another life priority area that is worthy of consideration. The relationships are life-long with bonds that continue to strengthen over the years. Family is very important, but it can be challenging due to various personalities as well as the multitude of broken homes and relationships in our world. Unfortunately, this is an area that is often short-changed when striving to build a "good life." I find this to be especially true for men. We have a tendency to over-invest in our jobs or businesses, and under-invest in relationships. This suggests that we see work as a challenge for us to overcome and defeat so that we can make the best living possible for our families. We invest a great deal of time and energy in this pursuit, which can become intoxicating, stimulating, stressful, and draining. It can also shape our identity if we are not careful. Have you ever been asked the question, "What do you do?"

The family is designed to help us grow and develop an understanding of how to live with and for others. There are issues in families from time to time but, at the core, most family members are there for each other. The challenge that we have in this country and our world is that the family is being broken apart and challenged. Almost 50 percent of marriages end in divorce. We have many single-parent households, which often result in one parent challenged to carry the load in terms of taking care of and providing for the children. This has a tendency to lead to children raising themselves. This can also happen in two-income households—if both spouses work, it can be just as difficult to balance work and family responsibilities.

I grew up in a home where my mother was at home, and my father worked hard to take care of my mother and four children. He was a janitor for an international automobile parts manufacturer. He would put in a full day's work, then come home and work in the garden. My mother took care of the home. She was a seamstress, a hairdresser, and served as a housekeeper. With regard to education, neither finished high school. They left school to work in an effort to support their families. They had a desire to raise us well, despite the challenges that they faced. Having parents who were committed and loved us was a blessing, and it has motivated me to be the best person that I can be and to find ways to make the world better rather than complain. Having a strong family is and has always been an important part of my life. I am thankful for my parents.

I am also thankful for my brothers and sister. I was the oldest of the four of us and often found myself assuming a leadership role, for which I was not prepared and probably did not handle very well. I worked to take the pressure off my parents as much as I could. We were close-knit, and spent the majority of our time in school and church. When we were not in school or church, we played with relatives and friends in the community. Some of the things that I learned as a child—with my brothers and sister—remain with me today. I learned to share, and I learned to respect and look out for others. As the oldest, I served as somewhat of a mentor—a role in which I am sure that I struggled. Having an intact family unit can be a blessing to the people in the family as well as others.

Family is a high-priority area, and I imagine it is at or near the top of your list. It is important that you define what family means to you and determine how you will serve and be there for those whom you love.

I had a son while in college, then eventually married and had another son. I have realized what my parents must have experienced when raising us. It is a blessing to be a parent; however, it is also a continuous learning process. I am very thankful that my wife was and is there to share love, responsibility, and support. That was especially true as I held roles that required frequent travel during a portion of my career. I would ultimately make sacrifices to be there for my family. That meant forgoing promotions and opportunities to be transferred to interesting places. Melinda and I made a conscious decision to provide stability for our son, Michael, and I am happy that we did. We moved from South Carolina to Ohio, and instead of climbing the ladder in the rat race, we made the decision to stay in Cincinnati and build a life here. This led to me leaving Michelin, a company for which I thoroughly enjoyed working, to take on a new role at Macy's. My time at Macy's allowed me to do meaningful work, grow, and develop new skills. However, more importantly, it allowed me to be there for my family and extended family as well.

You have heard a little about my family and home. How is this area of life for you? It is critically important that each of us make family and home a priority regardless of our current situation. The relationships that we have with the people we love are vital. As we learn to love and lead our families well, we grow and strengthen our ties. A strong family can provide a solid foundation that will prove helpful as we work to live out our purpose on earth. As you assess where you are in this area, do not lose heart if you are not where you would like to be. Make home and family a priority, and set goals that align with what you would like to see. Then take the necessary steps to love and serve your family in a way that will strengthen weak relationships and enhance strong ones.

HEALTH AND FITNESS

Another high-priority area is health and ensuring that we are taking care of the physical component of life. As is true in the other areas, health and fitness take work and intentionality. They also require a certain level of discipline, long-term think-ing, and an understanding that the work we do today can em-power us to be effective in other areas of life. When I hit the virtual wall, I realized that I had neglected my health. I am a former athlete who prided himself on being physically fit. As I entered responsible adulthood after marriage, I lost sight of the importance of health in many respects. I ate too much and moved too little. This led to gradual weight gain that I did not realize was happening because I neglected to get on the scale. As I gained weight, I started to have back and knee pain. How-ever, I never connected the two. I just kept moving forward until I was forced to stop and take care of myself.

Growing up in the South, we had tremendous food. I loved fried chicken and almost all other fried foods. I also enjoyed hamburgers—the bigger the better—and sweets galore, with honey buns as my favorite treat. When I was young, this was not a big deal, but as I grew older it became an issue. Many gatherings with family and friends occurred around food. Fun, festivities, and fellowship were almost always accompanied by food. We did not consider the impact that our cultural food choices were having on our health. Also, we did not have the wealth of information available to us today, nor did we have the internet. In some ways, this continues to affect many families. Very little is taught about the negative effects of poor diet and lack of activity on the body. Sadly, when we look at health statistics, especially for many different minority and ethnic groups, we see the disproportionate impact of various diseases and conditions. The COVID-19 crisis is an example. Many people have contracted the virus and succumbed to it. Unfortunately, People of Color (POC) are being affected at a disproportionately higher rate. Therefore, a key priority should be understanding how cultural conditioning and habits can influence our health.

A talented young leader, who is a POC and an exercise and diet professional, shared with me his concern for his family. He recently had an uncle pass away, which really bothered him. He was aware of his family's diet choices, but he did not know what to do about them. Large amounts of sweet tea and other unhealthy choices were devastating his family and many other people. He made a commitment to share some of the things that he had learned with his family and others. Sadly, the problem is not concentrated in just one region; it is affecting the entire country. This is just one example of conditioning, but it is an important one that deserves my attention and yours. In communities that are underserved, the problem is even more significant. Many residents of inner-city, rural, and Appalachian communities do not have the resources to purchase healthy food, which is often more expensive than unhealthy choices. Moreover, many who face financial challenges do not have grocery stores in their communities—they live in food deserts. This is a very sad reality for a country like the United

States. We each have an opportunity to help change this situation by sharing information, giving to charitable causes that support initiatives focused on ensuring change in this area, or joining an organization working to address these issues.

Another area related to health is exercise. It is imperative that we make time for exercise, both physical and mental. We must move our bodies by following some type of exercise regimen, or by merely getting up and walking. Join a group or partner with family or friends, and hold each other accountable for walking or running a certain distance or amount of time several days a week. Burning calories and getting your heart rate up can pay dividends as you live, lead, and serve in a world filled with stress and competing priorities.

Another extremely important factor is mental health. In the midst of the COVID-19 pandemic, we are seeing a tremendous increase in mental health issues. There is isolation, depression, anxiety, job loss, and fear of illness, along with racial strife. We are unsure of what is going to happen next. Add to these some of the weather issues that we have recently experienced, such as tornadoes, hurricanes, torrential rains, and forest fires. Each of us should make managing stress and our mental health a priority. Exercise, along with the spiritual and ethical components of life, can be helpful in this regard.

Guard your heart and mind, and take steps to protect your emotional and mental health. If you are at a place where you need help, please get it. You can work with your local healthcare system. Alternatively, there are many people and organizations willing to provide support, treatment, and assistance if needed. You can also utilize the National Suicide Prevention Lifeline, which is available 24 hours a day.

Taking the time to clear our minds is important. Thoughts are constantly running through our heads, and many times we end up thinking about what we should be doing or should have done rather than being present in the moment. The term *mindfulness* is a buzzword now, but I feel that this issue goes beyond that. It is important to slow down so that we can center and focus on what matters most. It is interesting to note how the COVID-19 pandemic has caused us to pause—for many of us, taking a pause feels awkward.

Melinda and I were once on a vacation in Europe, and I met a retired pastor who coached other pastors. He shared that he spends time in centering prayer. He spends time listening to the voice of God rather than talking. If you are someone who thinks that mindfulness or meditation is an Eastern thing, I encourage you to try centering prayer.[1] Make it an imperative to focus on your health in this way. Without doing so, it is difficult to focus on any other priorities.

To achieve our goals and realize our true potential takes energy. Energy comes from taking care of our physical and mental health. This fact is often neglected as we excitedly move toward what is important to us. How many times have we heard someone say that they are too busy to exercise? Many of us have probably heard it and perhaps said it as well. However, we must take the time for self-care. When we do this well, we find that in addition to having more energy, we are better fo-

---

[1] You can Google information on it and you can also find a few books that address this particular subject.

cused and, will ultimately, accomplish more. Additionally, we feel more present and have the fortitude and the energy needed to keep pressing forward.

There have been times in my life where I have burned the candle at both ends, and I have had people who reported to me do the same. I eventually adopted Jim Rohn's quote, "Work harder on yourself than you do on your job," and began sharing it with others. It was particularly insightful for a team of wonderful leaders that I had the opportunity to lead and supervise. When I initially said this to the team members, all of whom were passionate about their work, they looked at me as if I was out of my mind. After internalizing this concept and employing it in their own lives, we saw tremendous improvements in both individual and team performance. We accomplished great results, and many of our team members and the team as a whole were recognized for their efforts and contributions. Having energy starts with taking the time to invest in the important priority area of health.

The other thing to consider with respect to health is that poor health can lead to increased expenses. It can be economical to be more discerning about our health. Healthcare costs are rising rapidly and many of these costs are passed on by hospitals and medical systems to companies, which makes it more expensive for employers to provide health insurance for their employees. Employers are now also passing on more of the cost to their employees. It is critically important that we find a way to make taking care of our health a priority.

Food is delicious. We have many wonderful restaurants in our world, and a huge variety of food is available. Unfortunately, what tastes good to us is often not good for us. Many of us grew up on tremendously tasty, but unhealthy, diets. Consider, for example, soda. I worked in a manufacturing plant for an international beverage company one summer as a forklift driver. It was a fun job and a refrigerator was available that was filled with all sorts of cold, carbonated beverages. I certainly drank my share, but what tasted good was not good for me. One day, I had severe back and side pain. I was not sure what it was, but it was painful! It continued until I finally decided to see a doctor. When I did, I was told that I had kidney issues that had been caused by drinking too many sodas. I was instructed by my physician to drink as much water as possible each day and avoid carbonated beverages. This was difficult to do, but I wanted to feel better, so I adhered to the doctor's orders. Lo and behold, I began to feel much better after a few days.

Health is something that should not be taken for granted. I encourage you to evaluate what you are putting in your body and to be selective about it. Some people live in food deserts and do not have access to healthy foods. I understand that, but if there is a will, there can be a way. Start wherever you can and make healthy choices today. Planting a small garden may even be an option.

In addition to the spiritual and ethical component of life, I feel that health is one of life's most important aspects. Be healthy and thrive. Longevity is something that many of us desire. There are many things related to health that we cannot control, but there are many things that we can. We are a blessed people living in the United States compared to many countries that have no access to similar resources. The important thing is to choose wisely when taking advantage of them. It is important to be intentional about making healthy choices.

MENTAL AND EDUCATIONAL

We can take advantage of education at any age, as there are so many choices for learning and growing without enrolling in a degree-seeking program. The internet has eliminated many barriers that have existed for ages. In the past, getting an education was not an option for many people, including African Americans and Indigenous Americans. There were few options, because the aforementioned groups were not considered capable of learning. I am thankful that our culture continues to change toward the positive in some ways. Unfortunately, the past conditioning remains. There are many disadvantaged groups who do not have a history of people going to college or getting a formal education, so they may not feel that doing so is possible for them. In some ways, that is part of my story.

All of us can take ownership of our own learning and adopt a growth mindset. If we have the desire and are willing to take the steps to learn, we can. Many communities, towns, and cities have libraries that go underutilized. There is a wealth of knowledge and information to be had from the resources housed there. It is said that many people do not read a book from cover to cover after finishing their formal education. There is a lot of truth to this. As I meet and interact with people, when the topic of reading comes up, I find that very few read for pleasure or learning. Many say they do not have time. This brings us back to the importance of being very clear on our priorities and scheduling them. If a person reads just one page a day of a book or books in which they are interested, they would read a total of 365 pages (which could be a few books) over the course of one year. Consistently taking small steps over a long period of time could lead to some very big steps. The education journey begins with desire. Reading is one way to intentionally self-educate.

Quite naturally, school is another way to obtain an education. If you are a young person reading this book, take your education very seriously. Take full advantage of your high school and, if you have the opportunity, college and post-college educational programs. Be intentional. Time flies—before you know it, this portion of your life will be behind you. Sometimes in schools, students devalue their classmates who are applying themselves. They give their classmates grief and do not encourage them, while they also fail to take their own education seriously. I witnessed this once when I visited an elementary school in an inner-city community. I spoke to the students and asked them about their career aspirations and dreams. I heard many answers, including rapper, athlete, movie star, pimp, and drug dealer. I asked why they aspired to those things, and the answer was that these people made a lot of money. At that point, a girl in the back of the room raised her hand and said that she would like to be a teacher. I was encouraged by her comment and desire, but became disappointed when a few of the other students started giving her grief for her choice. I was surprised and asked the students why they acted the way they did. Sadly, no one had an answer. Conditioning of this type can affect young people throughout their lives if nothing changes. During my time with the students, I made the case for taking education very seriously, setting goals, and thinking beyond current circumstances. I reminded them that it is important to think with your own mind and to be okay with going against the grain. This can be challenging because everyone wants to be accepted. It takes courage to be different.

College has become cost-prohibitive for many people, and some say that college is no longer worth the cost. Some are of the opinion that colleges train you for the jobs of the past and not the jobs of the future. College is expensive, but I do not agree with the assertion that college is not worth it. I feel that college can be essential.

I am a first-generation college graduate. I attended college because I wanted to learn and to continue my participation in athletics. I was fortunate that I got to do both. My experiences at Mars Hill University forced me to learn and grow, not just as a student but also as a person. It was not easy, but it was certainly worth it. I found the liberal arts curriculum to be very appropriate for me. I was taught *how* to think, not *what* to think. During my time in college, my character strengthened and my confidence grew, both of which proved invaluable as I transitioned to the workforce.

Education is expensive, but there are many grants and scholarships available if one has an interest in pursuing a college education. In addition, there are many online options that are not as cost-prohibitive as a residential college. Also, there are community colleges for the first two years. Moreover, there is a tremendous need for people in the skilled trades. In my community work, I have realized the significant talent shortages in these areas. Many companies offer tuition reimbursement for employees pursuing additional training. I was very fortunate that one of my employers was willing to pay the full cost of my master's degree program. There are many options. The most important thing is to clarify your educational goals. Why do you want to get an education beyond high school? What type of education do you want to obtain? A compelling desire can be the motivation to take steps that may propel you forward.

Education and learning can also be informal, and this is one of the best ways to grow. This could entail learning through conversations with others, which takes a willingness to listen. If you are willing to connect with others who have experience and expertise in a field to which you aspire, you can learn concepts that will help you on your journey. This type of practical experience and wisdom can supplement other types of learning that you undertake, such as school or online learning. This practical type of interactive learning is something that I wish I had taken more advantage of early in my career. Unfortunately, as a young high school student, I did not have access to people in the career field in which I was interested. Therefore, with encouragement from my mother, I made the decision to read. I read everything I could get my hands on. As I look back on that time, I'm very happy that I did. Reading took me to places we could not afford to go physically. I learned things that charted my path, and it is that path that I am still on today. In college, I gradually learned to take even more advantage of this wonderful mode of learning, and I came to understand the importance of informal learning. I sought out mentors, and had the opportunity to meet with people who provided information and insights that were helpful as I made the decision to pursue and maximize various opportunities.

Ultimately, I realized that my growth and development were my responsibility, and mine alone. These were not things that someone else was going to do for me. I had to take action, which meant prioritizing this as an important area of life and ensuring that it was on my calendar—if something is on the calendar, it often gets done. I also had to crystallize my thinking and set goals. After setting goals, I needed action steps and support along the way. I made the decision to pursue a master's degree while continuing to handle my demanding job with Michelin. At the time, I had a lot going on in my personal life. It was a wonderful opportunity because the company would pay for my advanced degree, so I enrolled and began the process. It was important to me, but it took a great deal of focus and sacrifice to accomplish. Had I not gotten my master's then, it may not have happened. I used my calendar to ensure that I was managing my time as best I could. Despite all of those efforts, it was still extremely difficult. I was driven by the fact that this was a goal that was important to me. I had realized that as an African-American leader in business, it was important that I maximized my educational opportunities. I persevered and completed the program. At graduation, I was honored to be recognized as Outstanding Graduate Student of the Year. That accolade was not one I had sought, but it was nice to be recognized for my efforts and for accomplishing a goal that was important to me. One highly-positive aspect was that I was able to relate what I was learning directly back to my job, which made my educational experience more engaging and relevant.

Ultimately, it helped me to be more effective and productive in my work. This was recognized by my employer and I noticed it as well. I was fortunate to have the full support of my immediate manager, who encouraged me to pursue my master's degree in business. He also urged me to take advantage of the tuition-reimbursement program, and even allowed me to carve out time for studying and coursework during my work time. My manager also did a wonderful job of modeling the way. During this time, he was actually working on a master's degree as well.

Growth is our responsibility. We cannot depend on our boss or anyone else to ensure our growth. Personal growth and development is a choice, and with each choice comes responsibility. Companies can create a supportive environment or provide programs and opportunities, but it is important for each individual to take advantage of them. Unfortunately, most people do not make personal development a priority. I have found that employees who are further down the hierarchy find it hard to adjust their schedules to take advantage of educational and enrichment programs. Most employers are focused on productivity and do not allow employees to be away from their jobs for very long. Moreover, at the senior-leader level, there is a presumption that you have "arrived," have it all together, and do not need time to focus on personal growth and development. It is easy to make this assumption and justify it through your actions—you have solved the self-leadership dilemma and do not need to focus on personal growth and development. We know that this is far from the truth. A leader has to model the way and be a champion for continued growth and improvement. Middle-level managers watch the senior leaders and take their cues from them. If they are not focused on personal growth, employees who are further down the hierarchy will not be either. This results in a society in which we have ineffective leaders in homes, communities, and organizations.

I made the decision as a young leader to work hard on myself, and I am glad that I did. As a benefits manager, I researched the number of people who were taking advantage of our tuition-reimbursement program that—at the time—paid for education in full. The assignment was to analyze benefit-program participation and retention after certificate or degree program completion. The results revealed that few employees left in the next five years. The more alarming statistic was that only a small percentage of the employees were taking advantage of the program. Again, we cannot rely on anyone else to take responsibility for our personal growth and development—each of us must own this responsibility. We must be clear on what we want, why we want it, and what we are willing to do to get it. We then need to take the necessary steps to move us toward that goal. Progress is rarely easy, but the rewards can be incredible. They can allow you to separate yourself from the pack from a performance standpoint. They can also equip you to effectively lead yourself, thereby preparing you to be a better leader of others.

The mind is a powerful thing. If you are not one already, I encourage you to become a life-long learner, and make investing time and energy in the educational and mental components of life a priority. Such an investment will prove transformational, pay tremendous dividends, and serve as a catalyst in helping you achieve your goals and dreams.

SOCIAL AND CULTURAL

The social and cultural aspect of life is a vitally-important area. This importance was modeled for me at a young age. My mother gave her time and love to others in our community, and my father gave vegetables from his garden and his time to help others. They both volunteered in church; my mother served as the treasurer, while my father, who enjoyed music, secured gospel groups to perform at church. I learned early on that it is not what you have, but what you give. We did not have much from a resource standpoint. However, my parents were willing to share love and what we had. As a child, I was encouraged to run errands for the elderly in my community without expecting anything in return. I learned a lot about my elders and developed relationships with them through my service. As a young person, I did not think much about this—I just did it. We each have something to give, regardless of how little or much we have.

As I grew up and attended college, the experiences related to serving others remained with me. During my college years, I got to know the president of my alma mater, Dr. Fred Bentley. I remember him inviting me to his office to meet with him. One of the questions he asked me when we were together was what I wanted to do when I graduated. I shared that I had an interest in banking, at which point, he immediately picked up the phone and called a senior leader of a bank in Charlotte with whom he had a relationship, which resulted in an interview for a job opportunity. Dr. Bentley also invited me to serve on a national blue-ribbon commission studying the future of the college. I said that I did not have much to offer as a young graduate with few resources and little real-world experience. He listened to my concerns, and then encouraged me to seriously consider the opportunity and to get involved. Ultimately, I did, and I learned a great deal from the experience. He cared and modeled a principle that stuck with me. We each have the opportunity to serve and give, and we should provide opportunities and encourage others to do the same.

Giving our time and resources to help others is extremely important. If there were more givers, our world would be a much better place. Think about your town or community. If it is anything like Cincinnati, there are tremendous opportunities. I think about the statistics in our city—many of the children live in poverty, and we have high premature birth and child mortality rates. In addition, many people do not have the basic necessities of life. Numerous organizations attempt to meet the local needs, but as their resources are limited, they need a great deal of help and support. I have had opportunities to serve in mentorship programs and inner-city resident support programs in addition to volunteering with organizations like Rotary International, which has an international/local focus.

With Rotary, I had an amazing opportunity to travel to Nicaragua with an organization called Matthew 25 Ministries, which was founded by a servant leader, Wendell Mettey. We visited Paso Real and Las Flores outside Managua. Prior to the trip, I thought I really understood poverty. However, after I had been there for a while, I realized that I really had no idea. There were very few older people in these communities and very few men. The homes were like paper huts with no floors. There was no running water and the children got one good meal each day. At the end of each day, we returned to a nice hotel in the city that was an oasis for foreigners, while the people in the community went back to their homes with no running water and no electricity. One thing that amazed me on this trip was the level of joy among the people there. They were all smiles, very genuine, and they seemingly had peace as well. They invited us to a church that lacked the conveniences you would find in the United States. They sang for us and gave us gifts. They were thankful for our visit and they wanted us to know it. Being the only African-American in the group and speaking very little Spanish, one thing that I noticed was that the people treated me as if I were one of them. As we walked across a courtyard, a little girl ran up to me, seemingly from nowhere, and called me "papa." This was funny to the group and to me as well, but there was also something intriguing about it. We went to this South American country to help get water to a village and to build a feeding center for the children living there, but it was clear that we got more out of our time there than they received from us.

There is a lot to be said for giving and having a heart of service. There are individuals and organizations in our local communities, country, and around the world that need our time, effort, energy, and resources. We each have something to offer and the world needs our gifts.

There are great benefits that come from giving. You will often receive more than you give in the form of gratification and satisfaction. In addition to those things, you will grow. This is especially true for young people who are just beginning their careers. Volunteer work with non-profits and service organizations offers many opportunities to take on roles and gain experience and wisdom. For example, I have taken on leadership roles in organizations such as Rotary, Habitat for Humanity, and the United Way. These experiences allowed me to give back and help others. They also allowed me to develop my leadership skills as I led others on committees and in other capacities. In situations like this, you learn the importance of building relationships and influencing others. You also learn about the power of serving with a group of people committed to a strong mission. They are altruistic, driven by their desire to make life better for others. They are also often unselfish people who are innovative and willing to give of their time and treasure.

Another benefit of giving of your time, energy, and resources is that you are afforded the opportunity to partner with people from whom you can learn. Many have experience from their time in multiple industries and functions. They are passionate about sharing with the organization that you are also supporting and they are willing to collaborate with you. As you work side by side, you learn things that you would not have otherwise been exposed. One reason that I wrote this book is because of the model and encouragement I received from a dear Rotary mentor and friend, Tom Powell. He was one who encouraged me to take on more responsibility within Rotary International. He also wrote a book himself and requested that I review it before it was published. We met periodically for breakfast, and he would always inquire about what was happening in my life. He shared his journey with me, and some of the wisdom that I gained during our time together I apply in my life today. In addition, I have crossed paths with many other people on this journey, whom I never would have met had I not made the decision to get involved and make a difference. One example is meeting someone while serving on another non-profit board who became a catalyst for a new career opportunity. I was not seeking a change, but that change occurred. We are individuals with a purpose and service is a big part of purpose. This gift of time, energy, and available resources has the potential to unite us. I am constantly reminded of this during the current COVID-19 pandemic. My hope is that we all evolve out of this crisis to be more united and focused on serving and making a difference in the lives of others.

It can be easy to fall into a mode of selfishness and "I am not my brother's keeper" thinking. We are put on this earth to serve people. As we serve others, we grow, and we put a stamp on the lives of others and the world that will continue long after we are gone. If we lived only for ourselves, life would be boring and unfulfilled. Think of living on a deserted island all by yourself. How would that feel? If you are anything like me, it would not feel very good. We have family, friends, and community that help shape us and provide opportunities for us to help shape them. A big part of our lives involves living out a purpose that involves people.

Service and community can be easy to forget. There are people who have neither food nor a place to live; there are also many who struggle to live in a way that allows them to maintain employment to provide for family members or others. Mental health, child poverty, and disease are major issues in our society. We have an increased number of children who live in poverty and women expecting children who have prenatal problems. The number of homeless people in our world keeps growing. Clarifying our purpose and considering the role that each of us may play in turning the tide is vitally important. We must also stop and consider our blessings, and how we can bless others. In my life, many people, including family members, have loved, served, and supported me. I saw this early in my life and even to this day, and I have a desire to be of service to others. This takes intentionality and focus, with the time invested certainly being worth it.

In the area of social and cultural, building relationships should be part of our focus. Here we want to explore the role that taking the time for social activities and friends can play in living out a full life. So often, work becomes the most pressing priority, and it crowds out everything else, like enjoying life and spending time with the people that we care about the most. That starts with family.

In my work life, I have known many people who were unwilling or neglected to take vacation time. This time would go unused or, if the company allowed it to be carried over, it would be carried over to the next year, just to be carried over to future years. In many places, not taking allocated vacation time is seen as a badge of honor or something of which to be proud. However, for a number of reasons, that is something that can be considered irresponsible because we all need a break. Jobs and small business ownership can be stressful and require a great deal of effort. In addition, if we are not careful, work demands have a way of adversely affecting our lives over a period of time. The key is to take some time away from your responsibilities, whatever they might be, in order to renew yourself and get reenergized. When you take time away, you often uncover new ideas and insights that are applicable to all areas of life that you would not have if you did not take time away from the constant grind. We should make it a priority to take appropriate amounts of leisure or vacation time. Moreover, if companies allowed us to donate time to someone else, we might consider donating it to a co-worker experiencing health or financial issues. Even then, it would be important to leave some time for ourselves.

There is a very big upside to taking time away for rest and renewal. Leaders and business owners often take work with them when they vacation, check their cell phones or watch every few minutes, or call into the workplace every day to see how things are going. They find it difficult to release themselves from the connection, often because they do not trust the people reporting to or working for them, or perhaps, they do not feel that anyone else can do the job as well as they can. This changes, however, when things such as illness, job loss, or business failure occur. The person and the job often suffer because the leader is forced to take time away, and/or has failed to develop others to feel empowered and able to take the reins. The key is to teach, train, delegate to, trust, support, and empower others, thereby ensuring that things will work seamlessly in your absence. This can also allow employees to grow, which can positively affect morale, which will ultimately strengthen the business. The other challenge here is that the leader is a model for his or her people. If he or she does not take time away, how will that affect employees' thoughts about being away? Likely, they will follow the leader and not take time off either. This replication of what they see modeled is not desirable. People can begin to assume that working tirelessly with little time off is expected. This may lead to burnout and dissatisfaction with work. It could also lead to turnover and, if people stay, low morale and low-quality work. Take time off and encourage others to do so as well. Our new age of technology can make it difficult to get away. The cell phone can be a blessing and a curse. I know a number of people who go on vacation and leave their phone at home. It may be hard to do and would take practice, but it is certainly worth trying.

This was a big challenge for me early in my career. I felt that I needed to be at work or available, and if I was not, then I was not doing my job to the maximum capacity. This approach led to stress, overwork, and almost a breakdown. After getting a little clarity and understanding of the importance of getting away, many things changed. I performed better, enjoyed increased time with family, had more energy, and even enjoyed my job more. I had a major breakthrough after traveling to the Middle East. My wife and I traveled to Israel, Turkey, and a few other countries on a two-week vacation with no cell phones. In my journal, I noted my desire to support Mars Hill University, which has a special place in my heart, and I shared my thoughts with my wife. After the vacation, we returned home and re-settled. The following week, I went back to work, where my executive assistant shared with me that she had received a call from my alma mater. A representative of the university would be in town soon and wanted to schedule a meeting with me. She said that she knew I had a great deal of respect and pride for my alma mater, so she had already scheduled a meeting on my calendar. I met with the visitor, Bud, and we thoroughly enjoyed our time together. This eventually led to my reengaging with the university, joining the advisory board and then the board of trustees, and ultimately becoming chairman of the board. For me, it paid to get away. I crystallized my thinking, realized an internal desire and need to serve, and received an opportunity to do so.

Life is truly about relationships. When you think of what will matter most to you at the end of your life, I am sure that it will not be what you have or the position that you have achieved in society. I would imagine that it is and will be people—the people you love and the lives that you have touched along the way. Time has a way of getting away from us if we do not focus. The things that should matter most can be put on the back burner as we move forward in life at a rapid pace, taking care of what is in front of us with little regard for what matters most to us. If you are like me, you have been there, you are there, or you will be there. However, it does not have to remain that way. Choose to make changes, modifications, and adjustments along the way.

It is important that we value each other because our time on earth is short. By taking the time to follow the Golden Rule in relationships, we ultimately end up living in a better world. As Helen Keller said so well, "Alone we can do so little; together we can do so much." I learned this through an accountability group that a friend, Mark Simes, invited me to join. Like many men, when I felt isolated, I tended to carry the weight of the world on my shoulders. When I leaned on and was transparent with a few guys who met consistently over a period of years, the pressure was released. We developed authentic relationships and held each other accountable. It was refreshing to have meaningful relationships with other men outside my family.

We should value relationships because they can end suddenly and quickly. My mother passed away suddenly in 2000, and it was a difficult time for me. There was no closure—my wife, son, and I were in Cincinnati. She, my father, and the rest of my family lived in South Carolina. I got the call and my life changed forever. Death and transition became real to me. It also taught me the importance of staying in touch and letting people know how you feel about them. I was fortunate that my mother and I always ended calls with "I love you." I know that I was loved and my hope is that she knew how deeply I loved her. We should take nothing for granted. Life is very precious and can end quickly.

With regard to taking nothing for granted, if we do not value and invest our time, it will be nearly impossible to focus on what matters most to us. Most of us are overcommitted and have too much on our plates. As a result, relationships and people often get the short end of the stick. The time that we waste cannot be retrieved. When it is gone, it is gone, so it is imperative that we do not take time or relationships for granted. We come into contact with people every day, beginning with our families. If you have children, you know how quickly they grow up and move on in life. It is the same with our parents and us. We cannot get those years back. Again, once they are gone, they are gone!

This is also true if you manage people. If you have people working for you, typically they look to you for leadership and direction. You have the opportunity to create an environment where they can excel and grow. Alternatively, you can create an environment where they operate out of fear and do not realize their true potential. Many leaders do not make the effort to invest in people because investing in people takes time. In the harried environments of both for-profit and non-profit organizations, few people seem to have enough time, or make the time, to consistently engage employees, or to provide feedback and positive reinforcement. Many people are disengaged and do just enough to get by. They have little allegiance to the organization or the people that lead it. By making people a priority and valuing each person and relationship, we can change the tide. As leaders, one of our greatest responsibilities is to create an environment in which people feel motivated, encouraged, developed, and held accountable. Sadly, very few leaders are actually taking on this responsibility, and the need for processes to change behavior in this area increases from day to day.

Networking and building relationships are other important areas when it comes to the social and cultural side of life. I have found it highly rewarding to connect with and get to know people who differ from me in terms of race, gender, ethnicity, and even culture and profession. There is so much to learn from and share with other people. As a corporate leader in my last role with Macy's, I made it a point to sometimes have a coffee, breakfast, or lunch with someone outside the company. Those breaks gave me opportunities to collaborate, strengthen my leadership skills, build relationships with others, and remain cognizant of the world beyond Macy's. These meetings resulted in some great ideas that I was able to apply personally and incorporate back on the job. Being intentional in this area also allowed me to collaborate with Jonathan Sams, a friend I met through community service. He served as an accountability partner as I went through the process of transitioning from the corporate world to entrepreneurship.

Building a network outside your current organization also allows you to establish relationships that may be helpful if you ever develop a desire to change career fields. I have interacted with many people who only started networking and building relationships after they were laid off or fired. In those situations, they were operating out of desperation, and sometimes appeared to be merely looking to get something rather than genuinely interested in building authentic relationships. Similarly, I have had friends who worked for major corporations and, after leaving those corporations, realized that their only networks were inside the companies they left. This did not happen intentionally—it was what everyone else did. Retirement is a new life, but it comes with rather difficult adjustments. It is very important that we "dig our wells" before we become thirsty, and build a network while still employed. Where are you today? If you find that you are singly focused, it is not too late to do something about it. You can speak with someone you know who connects well internally and externally, or you can hire a coach. I urge you to make the social and cultural area of life a priority and to be intentional about giving, serving, and building deep and lasting relationships.

CAREER AND BUSINESS

When we are young, we often dream about the day we will be old enough to get a job and earn our own money. We are often asked, "What would you like to be when you grow up?" As children, we find our primary models of occupations in our parents. You see one or both parents go off to work each day to earn a living and support the family. We are encouraged to study hard so that we can prepare to go out and get a job to earn a living. The assumption is that this is something that we are all supposed to do.

This thought evolves into an assumption that success is attached to earning a living and achieving as much as possible. We are often conditioned to follow the model of others, regardless of their profession or role. We do this without having defined "success." We are motivated to work at a job or to start a business without a clear understanding of whether or how doing so aligns with our purpose or gifts. How many times have you spoken with someone who held a dissatisfying job for many years in order to earn a living, but was unwilling to make a change? They were locked in a situation with retirement as the only end in sight—if they made it that far. This type of commitment and dedication is noble, but in our day and time, it is seen less often. The younger generations have a somewhat different focus and seem open to changing jobs much more frequently. They appear to be looking for more from a job than just a paycheck.

This mentality may have resulted partly from the Great Recession of 2008, and it will likely be even more pronounced as we move through the COVID-19 pandemic. Some young people came of age watching their parent(s) being laid off after many years of commitment, with little to show for their time with the company, business or organization. There is more of a desire to do purposeful and meaningful work. Young people are often much more open to creating businesses and to learning, earning, and giving. The question often becomes how to do this after graduating with a large amount of debt from student loans? From where do you get the money to get started? The "old fashioned" way is not as bad as it is said to be. A job can be a means of achieving your goal.

A job in any organization offers the opportunity to do more than earn a living. It can also offer you an education on work and life issues, such as responsibility, expertise, managing relationships, and teamwork. If a person excels at their work, they are often given increased responsibility. This can be wonderful for the ego and your wallet, but it can be a challenge when your time and your priorities are not aligned, and when you are unclear on what is most important to you. Work can drain your mental, physical, and emotional energy. It helps to become clear on your goals in all areas of life and to be efficient at investing your time, rather than merely managing it.

A normal workday is eight hours of a twenty-four-hour day. If you are not careful, eight can easily stretch to ten, twelve, or more. Finding a way to effectively plan your month, week, and day is really important. This is true regardless of the type of job you have or the responsibilities that you have been given. I experienced this as a young executive and it became even more difficult when I had people reporting to me. I realized that I set the stage and created the environment for the team. They modeled my behavior. If I worked all of the time, the assumption was that they needed to as well. I have been in situations where coworkers would not leave work until the supervisor left out of fear or a desire to find favor with the supervisor. I have learned that it is not the responsibility of the boss to steward my time—or yours. The key is to be clear on the expectations and plan well so that you can meet those expectations during the time that you dedicate to work. If you do that well, then you can move on to other things in life that are probably much more important to you.

There are many tools that you can use for time management. The cell-phone calendar has become very popular. I use it as part of a process, but the challenge is that it is hard to only check my calendar—I tend to also check email and social media, and probably send a text or two. These tools have a tendency to take time away rather than give you more. I now use a calendar or planning tool that is similar to the old Franklin Planner. It is called a My-Tyme Success Planner and was developed by Leadership Management International, the organization I mentioned earlier that was started and built by Paul J. Meyer. If you have not heard of him, I recommend that you look up the company. His organization, with which I am affiliated, offers great tools that you can use to become more effective and productive. To manage your time well, you need a tool and a process that will be helpful. An investment in optimizing your time will pay dividends many, many times over the course of your life. If you don't currently have an effective calendar tool, I encourage you to find a system that will work well for you.

In your career, strive to be excellent in all that you do. It is also good to be open to challenging and growth-oriented assignments and even to changing jobs. This is also true for lateral moves. If your desire is to start your own business, it will not hurt to get vital experience in all the important areas of a business or industry. During my corporate career, I had the opportunity to gain valuable experience in diverse areas of business. The areas were operations, human resources, finance, sales, and project management. I did this while working in the textile, waste, financial services, automotive, and retail industries. This has proven helpful, as my wife and I now own and are running two businesses. As a business owner, the wide range of experience that I received has equipped me to better support my clients, as I am able to consider their organizational needs in a broader way.

As a corporate executive, taking on challenging and diverse assignments kept me stimulated. In addition, I was equipped to better understand the overall organization and the various segments of the business. My focus was not just on my department—I could consider the decisions that we made in the context of the overall organization and economic environment. It took some level of risk to make a decision to get a broad range of experience, but as I look back, I am glad that I did. I found the process stressful in some ways, because I was always challenged to learn new material and relate to different sets of people and circumstances. However, I can honestly say that I am a better leader today because I took the risk.

Unfortunately, I did not consciously travel this path. The path ebbed and flowed. I also found myself on this path because of my desire to learn as much as I could and to not miss out on any opportunities. No clear path was laid out before me that I could follow, as I did not have a family history of people working in professional environments. As such, I created my career path through a mixture of experimentation and curiosity. I had a few informal mentors along the way, but most of them were people who were experts in a particular field, and they had invested a significant portion of their careers in progressing up those particular ladders. I was headed down a similar path in human resources until I was selected for a high-potential program during my time at Michelin, which challenged me to work on projects outside my areas of comfort and expertise. That opportunity exposed me to other divisions of the company, such as marketing, sales, and logistics. With my previous experience in the organization, I was able to learn but also to provide input based on my observations and analyses.

With any career, there has to be an understanding that we do nothing alone. It takes the help and encouragement of other people to have a positive impact on any organization or community. Finding ways to build a network of people is very important. Napoleon Hill, in his book *Think and Grow Rich*, refers to a "mastermind" concept. He believes that you are only as strong as the people with whom you associate and surround yourself. Every person should be intentional about creating a life and relationships beyond their jobs. In this era of competition, jobs are not as secure as they once were; therefore, it is your responsibility to connect with people outside your organization while you are still working. These individuals could provide a unique or external perspective on a work-related problem that you may be experiencing. Growth requires thinking beyond who and where you are today. It requires being a visionary and finding ways to develop yourself that will pay dividends during your career and beyond.

FINANCE AND MONEY

The financial area of life is also very important, but it can also be one of the most challenging. We live in a world that is driven by economics. As a result, it is important for everyone to become financially literate and understand how to handle his or her hard-earned money. Unfortunately, there is no intentional effort to educate the public regarding money. Very little attention has been paid to financial literacy in our educational system, and as a result, most people struggle to answer basic money-related questions. Basic financial and money-related principles should be integrated into the curriculum of every school.

I grew up in a home with few financial resources. Nevertheless, my parents modeled stretching whatever they had and getting the most out of it. They raised four children in what started out as a four-room house. They added on to it over the years, taking it up to five, then six rooms. My father earned an income from his job, and he and my mother strategized on how to budget what he, and in some cases, she earned to make ends meet. I would often pay bills and run errands for them.

For many years, we used only cash—no checking account. This was my introduction to the importance of and need for money. My goal was to always bring back the correct change. For a time, my mother served as the treasurer at our small church. She took the collection after church and was responsible for taking it to the bank. In addition, she voluntarily took responsibility for helping to keep the books. The means of administering the finances was not very sophisticated by today's standards, but it worked. As a young child, I accompanied my mother to the bank from time to time. She challenged me to learn about and become comfortable with math and money. At the time, I did not understand it, but she was focused on helping and encouraging me to learn the basics so that I would one day be financially literate and comfortable managing my own finances.

As I grew older, I realized that there was no training in school on how to manage personal finances. Most of the people in my community and at school, whether high school or college, focused on earning and spending. Those in my community who saved did so utilizing passbook savings accounts. At that time, pensions existed. Therefore, in addition to Social Security, many people relied on pensions or some type of profit-sharing plan for their retirement. The passbook savings account was interesting, and saving for Christmas was the big thing. The premise was that you put money in the bank at very little interest and you took it out at Christmas time to purchase gifts for others. What was actually happening was that many were making the right decision to save. Unfortunately, the bank loaned that money to others at a relatively high interest rate and made a profit on the hard-earned money of the savers.

That was true then and it is true now. However, it is a process that most people do not understand or think about very much.

This was also evident with insurance—an industry with a history of discrimination. As far back as the late 1800s, companies were valuing policies held by Black adults at one-third the value of the same policies held by Whites. I did not understand the depth of this discrimination at the time, but as a young person, I noticed a discrepancy in my community. Many people who had insurance were sold low face value whole life insurance policies. They paid small monthly premiums for a minimal amount of coverage. The premiums for these policies seemed to be collected weekly by the agents. Term insurance policies, which are relatively inexpensive for larger amounts of coverage compared to whole life, were rare to non-existent. There was little understanding of how to utilize insurance appropriately for estate-planning purposes. Insurance was viewed as a way to cover burial expenses, which in all likelihood could have been saved for in ways that better benefited people.

In addition, many local department stores had layaway programs that allowed customers to put merchandise on hold, which the store kept until it was paid for in full. There was no interest charged because the merchant held onto the merchandise. After a series of small payments over time, the customer was able to take the item home after the full cost had been paid. Wonderful people were working hard to earn their money, while banks and retail stores were doing what was in their own best interest and certainly not to the benefit of their customers. Moreover, few families had a good understanding of basic financial or economic principles. Again, organizations were reluctant to take the steps to provide educational programs, and few people had an understanding of how to get an education on their own. As I reflect on this, I find that it is no different from the situation today, except the dollar amounts are higher due to inflation. The financial-literacy void adversely affects financial stability as well as the ability of minorities and others to build generational wealth.

The financial area of life is extremely important. It can provide the means to meet the needs and wants that we have in other areas of life. Instead of money ruling us, we can rule and manage it. As spiritual beings, we have the ability to subdue the earth, and that includes money. We have the capacity to use it well. It will certainly take some training, which is available, but you have to seek it out, take the time, and make the effort to learn.

Unfortunately, few of us have or will ever reach our true potential in life, and that is certainly true with respect to money. If it were not true, most of the wealth would not be concentrated with an extremely small percentage of the population. I have come to define financial success as the ability to live the remainder of your life without outside help, working when you choose, but doing so only if and when you desire. In my mind, that is true freedom because you are in control of your time. I have heard freedom referred to as "the new wealth." This kind of wealth is available to all of us. No matter where you are currently, you have the ability to achieve this freedom.

The first question you are probably asking yourself is *how*? My answer is to educate yourself and clarify your goals. Spend less than you earn, and invest the remainder at a reasonably good interest rate. That sounds relatively simple, but it can be difficult to achieve, especially if you are doing it on your own. Financial advisors, investment clubs, or accountability partners are good options. No matter what you do, it is important that you connect with people who have your best interest at heart and whose values align with yours. You should also take responsibility for your own financial education and not abdicate your responsibility to others.

Money can be viewed as an idea. The hard-earned cash that you may have in your hand right now is not real, and it really is not worth anything without the faith that we all have in our economic system. The subject of economics is something that I would encourage you to study. The supply and demand of goods are big parts of the process. The system counts on consumer spending to keep it going. The majority of the messages that we receive on a daily basis are often about spending to get something or to feel good about ourselves. To go against the grain takes self-discipline. You must have the discipline to walk away from some items that you want but do not need. To do this, it helps to have a budget and a good understanding of your long-term goals, dreams, and desires. To develop such an understanding, you often need help from someone who is unbiased and focused on your best interest. This can be difficult to find. In fact, after getting input from a number of people including a wonderful person and friend, Jimmy Macon, I decided to start my own financial-planning firm to help fill the void in this area.

My life's journey, experiences, and exposure led me to getting the CERTIFIED FINANCIAL PLANNER™ or CFP®

designation, that is often considered to be the Ph.D. of financial planning. I studied business in undergraduate and graduate school, including economics and corporate finance, but in some ways, it was all theory. I had difficulty understanding how to practically apply the principles in my life. I was informed, but my curiosity was not satisfied. It was not until I began to work in the corporate arena and interact with adults who were not making smart decisions with money that I was able to apply theory and take action. I met a gentleman who introduced me to the dividend reinvestment plan (DRIP) method of investing. This was after I reached out to a brokerage/investment advisory firm, expressing an interest in opening a brokerage account, and was told that I did not meet their minimums or asset requirements. This was surprising, because I did not know that anything of the sort even existed! Nevertheless, I was not deterred. I invested in a DRIP. Melinda and I were saving in company plans, but we had not thought through things like asset allocation. That was, not until I had the opportunity to manage a benefits office and a credit union at a manufacturing facility for a few years during my working career. This was an eye-opening experience. I received training and was introduced to the institution that was the administrator of our 401(k) plan.

Working as a benefits manager allowed me to see that many people had very little understanding of the value of money, or how to properly save and invest it. I would often sit in the benefits office and the credit union while the administrative staff interacted with the employees who flowed through on a daily basis. This helped me understand that people make poor decisions regarding their money due to a lack of education and knowledge. I noticed that people making average to above-average incomes were spending money on things that they did not need, often with money they did not have. As a result, bankruptcies and the use of 401(k) funds to purchase non-essential and depreciating items were not unusual. I invited a financial advisor in to provide education. This helped to a certain degree, but the people needed more. My intense desire to help people in this regard led me on a journey to get my securities and insurance licenses. I joined the independent non-profit corporation called the American Association of Individual Investors (AAII) and devoured as much information as I could with the intent to share it. Prior to all of this, I served in a human resources management role during a time of organizational downsizing. As a human resources leader, I had the opportunity to interact with many employees affected by the downsizing, which taught me that there were and are no guarantees of a job. Consequently, it is imperative that people manage their resources well and plan for emergencies.

This experience motivated me to move forward in increasing my own financial literacy and finding ways to help others as well. I joined a large financial firm on a part-time basis, intending to help people and grow my business. However, I soon realized that the focus was more on gathering assets and charging commissions than on helping people. Initially, this experience disappointed me, but disappointment shifted to motivation, and it motivates me to this day. As a result, I stepped away from the financial industry for many years until in 2017 I started my own firm, Kelly Financial Planning. My focus is on educating and helping people make smart decisions with their money. I provide hourly and project-based services and do not sell products nor receive commissions from any brokerage house or mutual fund company. This allows me to do what is right by my clients and do what is in their best interest. It also allows me to live out my mission and purpose, which includes helping people grow to become all that they are created to be. I also get to help my clients create plans that will allow them to experience their dreams of freedom. We all have the ability to achieve our life goals and financial success. However, it will take work and, probably, some help, but it is possible. Having a financial plan, regardless of how simple, is a great place to begin.

The basic elements of a financial plan are budget and cash flow, savings, investment, insurance, education, retirement, and estate planning. All of these areas are important and are addressed based on your goals and needs.

A huge barrier to financial success is often one's money mindset. That mindset is made up of experiences beginning in childhood and is the result of conditioning. What did you see and experience in the places where you lived, worked, and played as a child? You develop a way of seeing money and the world based on past experiences. If you were around people who spent everything they made, overspending may be a challenge for you. If you were around people who were serious about planning and investing, you may be disciplined and have a long-term perspective. Unfortunately, financial literacy and good stewardship of money are not the norm. A tremendous number of sources tell us that we live in a country where people retire with very few resources.

It does not matter where you begin. You deserve to have financial success and the ability to manage your money well. Start by assessing your money mindset and developing a financial plan. Money can cause a great deal of angst and stress. Some people avoid this stress, and some people delegate it to others with few or no controls in place. Some people make an attempt to manage their money themselves, but many give up out of frustration or because they find it too complicated. I believe that anyone can learn to manage his or her money well, but doing so takes thoughtful planning and continuous reviews. The work begins with self-education, learning, and reading financial information widely and often. You can also join various groups, like the American Association of Individual Investors (AAII) or other organizations committed to investor education. In addition, you can take advantage of employee benefits information provided by your employer. The important thing is to find a way to learn. Another step that can be helpful is to find a mentor and collaborate with them. There are many people who would be happy to share what they have learned with those who are interested.

One primary aspect of money that we need to understand is cash flow. How much money is coming in and what am I doing with it? Where is it being spent and on what? You must know where your money is going and why. The 55/25/20 rule can be helpful with managing cash flow and your money overall.

This rule is easy to follow:

- 55 percent of your income should be allocated to living expenses and essentials, such as rent or mortgage, groceries, and transportation.
- 25 percent of your income should go to savings, investments, paying off debt, and charitable giving.
- 20 percent of your income should go toward the things you want but do not necessarily need.

An important note: the essential and flexible spending percentages are the maximum; you always want to try to go *below* these percentages if you can. Obviously, the things in your "want" category are going to be what you want to limit the most; essentials and savings—in most cases—should take precedence. However, everyone has a preferred spending method according to their financial objectives.

In addition to this rule, it could be beneficial to partner with a fiduciary financial advisor—someone who is objective and commits to keeping your best interest in mind—to develop a comprehensive financial plan. This process will help you to clarify your life and financial goals, and to detail the action steps necessary to achieve financial success.

Whatever you do, do not let your money control you. Find a way to become the master of it.

CHAPTER 6

SET AND ACT ON MEANINGFUL GOALS

———

Relatively little of note has been accomplished without goal setting. We should clarify and consider the desired direction for our lives and develop clearly-written goals in the most important areas. Before writing goals, we should prioritize the areas of life we reviewed based on what is most important to each of us individually.

Goal setting is extremely important, but is often misunderstood and omitted. The Cambridge Dictionary defines goal setting as "the process of deciding what you want to achieve, or what you want someone else to achieve over a particular period." Goal setting appears to be a simple concept; however, speaking from experience, it can be quite challenging. There were many times in my life when I lived without utilizing the process. My life changed dramatically when I began to plan, embrace, and set clearly-written goals.

In the book, *What They Don't Teach You at Harvard Business School*, Mark McCormack describes a study of MBA program graduates conducted by Harvard University from 1979-1989. They were asked the question, "Have you set clear, written goals for your future and made plans to accomplish them?" Three percent had clearly-written goals and plans, thirteen percent had goals but not in writing, and eighty-four percent had no specific goals at all. Ten years later, the three percent who had clearly-written goals earned ten times as much as the ninety-seven percent who did not have clear goals.

The essential steps in the goal-setting process are as follows:

1. Establish SMART goals aligned with your personal mission statement in all areas of life. You must be clear on your desired future.
2. Develop action steps for each goal, and consider the benefits to be gained from moving forward and the losses to be avoided.
3. Add deadlines for action and determine who will hold you accountable for achieving them. Coaching and accountability are important parts of the process. Identify a competent coach or an inspiring mentor.

My hope is that we will make it a priority to live meaningful and intentional lives. Being among the three percent who have clearly-written goals should be our aim. There is power in goal setting, but we will only realize it if we are intentional about setting goals, embracing them, and taking action. If we do this well, we will ultimately achieve goals that really matter, and we will lead more meaningful and productive lives.

UTILIZE A GOAL-PLANNING SYSTEM TO ACHIEVE GOALS

It is one thing to set goals and another to take action to move toward achieving them. A goal is often a dream without a plan. Paul J. Meyer of Leadership Management Incorporated developed a wonderful tool called a goal-planning system. The system covers seven steps that are critical to achieving goals.

1. Set a goal. It is important to ensure some specificity when setting goals. They should be as clear as possible.
2. Determine benefits from achieving the goal and losses to be avoided from not achieving the goal. You want to consider the ways in which you will be helped or harmed by achieving or not achieving the goal. Think through the pros and cons.
3. Consider possible obstacles and solutions. With any move forward or attempt to make progress, there will be obstacles. How will you address them? It helps to think through this up front and determine the solutions to those obstacles. This can serve as encouragement and motivation to move forward with confidence because you have already processed

how you will handle the challenges that may present themselves.

4.   Develop action steps (target, review, and completion dates). Hold yourself accountable for taking the steps necessary to move forward. Goals are nothing without action, just as faith is nothing without works. We can plan forever, but no real progress is made until we take action.

5.   Select a method of accountability. The document also lists or allows one to list chosen methods for accountability. It helps to share your goals and to have someone to hold you accountable. This person can, for example, be a family member, mentor, friend, or boss. The key is that you trust the person, and the relationship is one in which they will be honest with you. It is also important that they care and have your best interest in mind.

6.   Determine methods of tracking progress. There are many methods for tracking your progress, but as mentioned, I prefer a planner book. I use the My-Tyme, which allows me to have everything in one place. I know all of my priorities, goals, action steps, and things that I want to accomplish. The system also includes a tool that allows you to track activities—on a daily basis—related to your monthly goals. In setting goals in all of the major priority areas of life, I find this tool to be invaluable. I was recently at a meeting where we were asked, "What is one thing that you would run back into a burning house to get

if all of your family members and most important belongings were already out?" For me, one of those things would be my My-Tyme. Electronic devices can also be effectively incorporated into the process.

This type of system allows you to dissect your goals and crystallize them. This is key to success in achieving a goal. If you are clear on the *what* and the *how* and if they align with your *why*, the possibility of achieving the goal increases. If we are going to take the time to set goals, we need to execute them well. Having a system like this can be very helpful.

Having timelines as to when you will take an action or achieve a goal is also an important part of the goal-setting process. If you set a timeline, you will find that you will have an accountability mechanism in place that will keep you honest. It will serve as a marker to remind you that action is needed, and it may also serve as motivation. I have established timelines in the past where some were too aggressive while some were too conservative. Both extremes were a problem. The timelines that were too aggressive resulted in my working too hard or not at all because I gave up, feeling that I could not achieve them. With timelines that were too conservative, I realized that I was not taking action with a sense of urgency. Many of those led to procrastination and not taking action at all. I realized the importance of building timelines that were reasonable and somewhere in the middle, and that did not put too much pressure on me. When I did this well, I sensed that I was making substantial progress and felt good about my path on the journey.

As a young leader, I worked with others and emulated their behavior, which resulted in activity and busyness. Sometimes the activities were considered "fun," but I have realized many were a waste of time—they were unproductive and did not contribute to personal or professional growth. Often, those activities were things like working long hours or establishing unrealistic schedules. I found myself doing things for people with little regard for why or what we were looking to achieve, and I was distracted and disconnected instead of valuing relationships. I have learned that clear thinking, which for me means goal-oriented thinking, allows us to maximize time, relationships and find more meaning in life.

It is exciting to set and achieve goals in the priority areas of life. When we busy ourselves with no direction, it can be extremely stressful and a true waste of time. This is true whether one is a student, a young employee, an executive, a business owner, or a retiree. I have experienced this myself, and I have coached and mentored others who were stuck in this cycle of busyness and lack of direction.

I think of students who are worried about getting good grades in college, but they do not want to miss out on the many other fun things happening at their institution of higher learning. They party all night, sleep all day, and study for a little while when they can work it into their schedule. They progress through college if they can avoid dropping or flunking out, doing just enough to get by. The experience goes by quickly, and they wonder why their grade-point average is stuck below 2.0. I also think of people who are beginning their careers and desire to climb the ladder of the organization for which they work or build a business to a sustainable level in a short period of time. They burn the candle at both ends, working to achieve something that is unclear. Sometimes they have a business plan, but in most cases they do not. They certainly do not have one for their own lives. This leads to a great deal of physical and mental stress because life tends to be about work and nothing more. I have also interacted with retirees who have given it their all during their corporate careers and reached a point where they can or must shift. As few baby boomers retire with enough money on which to live, they experience stress as they attempt to make ends meet. For other retirees who do not work and do not face financial challenges, the question is what they should do with their time. At this stage of life, many people feel that they are past their prime and do not have anything of value to add to our society or the world. This can lead to a feeling of helplessness or even hopelessness. Goal setting can help renew one's mindset and broaden life's meaning. If we combine goal setting with a clear understanding of purpose, a vision of the future, and a clear mission statement, goal setting in the priority areas can be transformational. We all deserve to live the lives for which we were created and to help others do the same. Taking a strategic approach to life is something that is not often talked about, but it is essential to our success.

If you are still unsure about whether goal setting is for you, I challenge you to give it a try. If you are like me, I am certain that you will find that you did not realize what you were missing. The process can add more meaning to your life in ways that are hard to imagine. Think about being more present and confident as you move forward on your life's journey.

You have a roadmap and some understanding of the road that you wish to travel as you move toward your destination. When you travel, it is nice to know that your GPS will get you where you want to go. Having the kind of detail your GPS provides takes the pressure off of traveling and allows you to relax. It is so easy to get busy without developing a good understanding of where you are headed. This was one reason I hit the wall relatively early in my career and life. I was not setting broad goals in all areas of life. I had a vague understanding of where I wanted to go in business, but I had not properly processed how I would get there. Again, that resulted in an increased focus on work and not much else. I was striving toward something that was unclear to me. Ironically, I have coached and worked with many people who were and are in the same place. They are driving toward something that requires an awful lot from them, but they are unclear on what or why. When you face burnout, business failure, or job loss, you are challenged to deal with the reality of where you are. If you do not deal with that situation properly, you will tend to seek out the next thing and start the process over again. This can result in health challenges, relationship challenges (including divorce), financial challenges, and more. It pays to crystallize your goals and develop a plan to achieve them. If doing so requires help, find someone to assist you along the way. Consider it an important investment in your life and future. You deserve it, as do those you love and serve.

ACTION STEPS

**You don't have to see the whole staircase,
just take the first step.**
— MARTIN LUTHER KING, JR., MINISTER, ACTIVIST

Goals are nothing without action. A goal is literally just a dream if you do nothing about it. Taking meaningful action is an important component of the goal-setting process. Goals are powerful but rarely realized when action is not taken to achieve them. Many people set goals and feel that the real work is done. Unfortunately, that is not the case. In many respects, the work has just begun. For example, having a goal of losing fifteen pounds is noble, but it will not be realized if specific action is not determined and taken. If you establish and execute specific steps, such as being more judicious about your diet and exercising a certain number of days per month, the likelihood that you will achieve your goal dramatically increases.

The process of taking action in a consistent and organized way follows setting goals in the most important areas of life. The timeframe will vary depending on the nature of the goal. I often encourage clients to think in terms of one-, three-, and five-year goals. We also discuss next-generation or legacy goals, which can have a long-term horizon of 200 years or more.

Create a definite plan for carrying out your
desire and begin at once, whether you are
ready or not, to put this plan into action.

—NAPOLEON HILL, AUTHOR

After goals have been established, an action plan should be developed for each goal. This process begins with evaluating the likely benefits of achieving a goal and the losses that should be avoided. This is followed by proactively thinking through potential obstacles and developing solutions for each one. Subsequently, each step necessary to achieve a goal should be listed along with a target date for completion. Preferences for managing accountability should also be considered.

Clearly setting meaningful goals and establishing action steps for achieving them can enhance performance and lead to personal fulfillment. Be proactive about taking action. Then, reflect on your progress and how well you did. As you take meaningful action and begin experiencing progress and success, you will likely feel motivated and inspired, and feel a sense of joy. I encourage you to make this a part of your life, and find ways to teach and encourage others to do the same.

**Our goals can only be reached through a vehicle of
a plan, in which we must fervently believe,
and upon which we must vigorously act.
There is no other route to success.**

—PABLO PICASSO, PAINTER

VISUALIZATION AND AFFIRMATIONS

What you see and believe is what you will be. There is a lot to
be said for having a clear vision of what you would like to see
and be. I did not understand this as a young person. I had desires as I continued to move through life, but I was uncertain
of how I would achieve them. A few of those desires were to
get a college education, play basketball in college, work and
travel overseas, work for a publicly-traded company, and work
for an international company. In other words, I had a vision. I
have come to believe in visualization—the creation of a mental
image of what you would like to achieve. For example, if you
would like to travel to a foreign country, develop a picture of
yourself in that country, enjoying the sights and sounds. It is
also a good idea to find a picture of what that might look like
and post it where it can serve as a reminder and a subconscious
motivator to assist you in moving toward this goal. Adding a
SMART goal to visualization creates a powerful combination
because, in addition to visualizing, you will begin to take actions that move you toward the goal that you are visualizing.
Let us again consider the overseas travel example. Having this
goal and envisioning it can motivate you to take action, such as
researching the particular place or speaking with a travel agent.

The action could also be letting your financial advisor know about your desire, and working with him or her to ensure that this is included in your plan. This will provide clarity on the steps necessary to save for this dream. You may also find yourself reaching out to people who have traveled to the location to get their perspective and insights.

In addition to visualization, it could be beneficial to write affirmations or statements as if you had already accomplished this goal. With respect to the trip overseas, you might write "I traveled to New Zealand and enjoyed the scenery and the delicious seafood dishes." This is a positive affirmative statement. You can write these statements and place them—in your line of sight—in various areas around your home. I worked with a coach who gathered a list of the things that I wanted to accomplish in my life and timelines for those goals. She then wrote a story of affirmation. She gave me an assignment: to read the affirmation story aloud ten times consecutively and record myself as I did so. The assignment also included listening to the recording each night for a minimum of thirty days while falling asleep. Prior to this, she read the story to me three times during one of our coaching sessions. This proved to be a great exercise for me because it incorporated spaced repetition, which subconsciously helped me internalize my goals and possibilities for achieving them. In addition, I was given a list of written affirmations, and asked to pick out the top eight and post them in places where they would be visible to me. Affirmations are powerful. If these kinds of exercises are not familiar to you, I encourage you to give them a try. If you need help, again, hire a coach or reach out to someone and ask him or her to serve as an accountability partner. Maybe you can help them, and they can do the same for you.

Many people will read these suggestions and forget about them. Those who are eager and truly interested in achieving their goals and self-actualization will probably try them. If you do, I am sure that you will find that it was time well spent and that you will have grown from taking this step. Don't stop there. Find a way to share what you have learned with someone else.

TIME MANAGEMENT

Time is a topic that receives a great deal of attention, but rarely will you find someone who feels that they manage time well. How are you doing in this particular area? Do you find that you have more than enough time to get things done? In a world of complexity and competing priorities, it can often be difficult to get everything done, and that is especially true for things that matter most to us. Living a full and meaningful life begins with improving your utilization of the precious commodity called time.

Time passes very quickly, and our minutes, hours, days, months, and years seem to "fly by." We often begin the year with New Year's resolutions focused on, for instance, losing weight, getting a promotion, or saving a certain amount of money. Rarely do we make resolutions related to improving our time management.

Time is really the only capital that any human being has, and the only thing he can't afford to lose.
—THOMAS EDISON, INVENTOR

Getting serious about better utilizing your time can lead to personal fulfillment and a life of more meaning.

It can be helpful to consider stewarding time as investing a precious and finite commodity. The three points below are things to consider as you intensify your focus on this important concept:

- **Prioritize priorities**—Rank the seven areas in the aforementioned "Wheel of Life" from the most to the least important. This will help you obtain clarity about which of the priorities you value the most.
- **Set goals and develop action steps**—Goals should be set in each priority area along with a few action steps that may be necessary to accomplish the goals. Focus on setting daily, weekly, monthly, and yearly goals.
- **Plan daily**—Your calendar will play a very important role here. Regardless of whether you use an electronic calendar or a "Franklin Planner," use it frequently. Plan at the end of each month for the upcoming month and plan for the upcoming week at the end of each week. You should also plan at the end of each day for the upcoming day. In addition, schedule your priorities on your calendar.

Getting comfortable with this process will take time. Nevertheless, the time you invest in improving in this area should yield great results. You will find yourself working on and allocating time to those priorities that matter most to you. This will lead to a higher level of productivity, personal fulfillment, and satisfaction.

Learn to say "no." Most people who ask you to make a commitment are, in a sense, salespeople who expect to hear the word "no." The average human being is exhausted owing to an abundance of commitments and obligations, many of which they have little passion. We have slim time-related margins and the demands on our time are high. We are challenged by the need to balance the many competing priorities in our lives. It can be difficult to refuse requests for fear of disappointing others. Most of us struggle with saying "no." However, focusing on improving in this area and becoming more comfortable saying "no" can be liberating.

Determine what your true priorities are and ensure that they align with your purpose. Prioritize your priorities and add them to your calendar. Then evaluate each request that you receive against these priorities. We each have only twenty-four hours in a day. According to the Centers for Disease Control and Prevention, the average lifespan for women is 81.2 years, while it is 76.4 years for men. It is critical that we not waste precious time attempting to please others while sacrificing our personal priorities.

Think of time as an investment rather than something you spend. A time commitment is an extremely important and finite portion of our lives. Do you easily say "yes" to investment opportunities without sufficient research or study? I hope not, because doing so could result in serious financial instability and loss. The same is true for our time—we should value it and help others understand the importance of doing the same.

DEALING WITH FAILURE

A serious conflict can occur if you are a risk-oriented person operating in a risk-averse environment. Such a situation can be confining and, among other things, often boring. I have experienced this at various points in my life. When I did, it was accompanied by little or no growth and/or limited use of my potential. I know others who have experienced this as well. You don't have to accept this situation. A solution can often be found by becoming more comfortable taking risks and accepting unexpected results. As Charles F. Kettering said, "Failures, repeated failures, are finger posts on the road to achievement."

Becoming comfortable with risk-taking and potential failure is possible, but it will take time and effort. We must first determine our personality regarding the various measures of risk-taking and acceptance of possible outcomes. Our personalities are developed over years and are related to experiences that have occurred throughout our lives. These experiences often result in subconscious mental conditioning. An example is someone who has been reprimanded at work for making a mistake or fired from their job. This could result in the individual "playing it safe" in the future in an effort to avoid a similar experience. As a result, little growth, if any, may take place, and their potential may be stifled and unfulfilled.

Connecting with a coach and getting feedback on behavior may help you begin the process of identifying conditioning and setting goals to break it. This can be accompanied by enrolling in a program that offers the opportunity for assessments and a development process occurring over a period of weeks or months. A strong process is one that includes goal-setting and action-step components. As you make progress, your confidence will increase as you find yourself taking more calculated risks. You may also become more accepting of decisions or actions that result in a lack of success in situations involving yourself or others. Ultimately, personal fulfillment and growth will occur as you shift toward a mindset of accepting and learning from both experiences, those that go well and those that do not.

What would happen if you sought out opportunities to fail or if you practiced failing? It would be scary, but it could lead to growth. I have found that when I decide not to take action in an effort to remain comfortable, I do not grow. I become stagnant and complacent. When I stretch myself and put myself into situations that I cannot control or that have outcomes I cannot predict, I embrace and foster skills or obtain the information necessary to succeed. However, if I do not succeed, I am then more open to learning about what went wrong.

One example of this is taking on big projects at work. Michelin considered leadership development extremely important and made it a priority. The company challenged high-potential leaders to step into areas and roles that they knew very little about. I, along with a few others, was selected for an extraordinary senior leadership development program that required completing both group and individual projects in areas of the organization that needed transformation. The company identified projects, assigned them to us, and placed us in specialty areas of the business about which we knew very little. As part of the process, we were encouraged, challenged, evaluated, and critiqued. Needless to say, there was a lot of pressure to get things right. What I have realized since is that the company planned for and expected failure. Our supervisors observed how we handled failure and what we learned from the process. They also wanted to see how we used the experience of failure to grow and to develop even better outcomes for the projects to which we were assigned. I worked hard on my assignments and often felt that I was "in over my head," but I found myself stretching, growing, and learning from things that went right and wrong. Ultimately, I finished the group and individual work with a certain level of success, and with the knowledge that failure was not fatal and that I could grow through it and achieve optimal results.

If you are not currently in a situation where failure is an option, you should rethink things because, in all likelihood, you will not experience the growth you desire and deserve unless there are obstacles to overcome. This is true in all areas of life. How did things work out when you first tried to ride a bike? If you are like me, it was not easy, and there was quite a bit of falling, getting up, and starting over again. How about learning to swim? For me, there was a certain level of fear—I did not trust the process or my abilities. This led to me getting water in my ears, nose, and mouth, and almost drowning at one point. Nevertheless, I had a strong desire to learn how to swim, so I kept trying. I learned from my mistakes and gained a little momentum and, eventually, signs of success. This led to my confidence increasing and I realized that I could swim if I put my mind to it. I decided not to let mistakes deter me from something that I wanted to do. I learned to swim and was able to teach a few others as well.

Have you ever heard someone say that they are the sum of all of their failures? I am one of those people. I have had a highly-rewarding life and career. I have traveled a path filled with uncertainty and no clear roadmap. As I mentioned earlier, although my parents grew up without many opportunities, they navigated life in a way that provided opportunities for my brothers, sister, and me. I knew that they wanted more for us than our culture and circumstances had allowed for them. As I learned more about all that they had experienced, I was even more motivated to succeed and make them proud. I studied hard and became a reasonably good student and athlete. Getting cut from the basketball team was a failure that propelled my success as a basketball player and a student in many ways. I wanted to play so badly that I worked hard for it and, ultimately, got a chance to attend college on a scholarship and to obtain a business degree. Playing basketball and risking getting cut again was a possibility, but learning from my failure and overpreparing allowed me to dramatically improve my skills and become a valuable member of every team that I have had the opportunity to join. Michael Jordan is someone who also failed, and you know his story. Do not fear failure—embrace it and be all right with becoming comfortable when you are uncomfortable.

I know that this can be difficult when it comes to work.

Work can be challenging and failure is often not rewarded. In fact, it may even be penalized. I have noticed that many people are afraid of failing, and I have seen many leaders who do not do a good job of teaching through failure. Leaders have a tendency to shut people down and, therefore, team members often do not grow. Both the individuals and the organizations in which they worked suffer in such situations. The customers suffer as well, because they do not necessarily get the best products or ideas available to meet their needs.

There are millions of people in organizations across the country who have, in essence, quit but are still on the payroll— they are waiting to be unleashed. Due to the fear of losing a job or not getting a promotion, they play it safe and are unwilling to disrupt things. A lot of this comes from the fact that they are not clear on their purpose, mission, and vision of success. It is important that we do the work needed to develop a strategic plan for life, which will help remove some of the fear of failure. For example, if you are worried about losing your job, it pays to get your financial house in order so that you can weather potential storms. This could also motivate you to take more risks or step into situations that may challenge you. Fear should not be feared—it should be embraced because as you move through it, you become more of the person you were created to be. Enjoy the journey, because you matter more than you know. Believe, trust, achieve, and help others do the same.

Have you ever been immobilized by fear? How did it feel? Was there anything good about it? At that time, did you feel that you were the best version of yourself? Many organizations are mired in cultures of fear. People do not want to make a mistake or do anything that may cause a problem, so they play it safe and work hard not to misstep. This stifles creativity, innovation, and the ability of the organization to grow and change. In this era of change at the speed of light, we need to be unleashed and the people around us need to be as well.

Take the time to determine where you are in relation to your view of and fear of failure. If it is not where you want to be, make the effort to change. Make the necessary adjustments today. You will be glad you did. This is something that we can all do, but it takes an understanding of what life means for you. Life is finite, so know your purpose and create a compelling vision of your future. Add to this a meaningful mission statement to navigate the many hurdles in life and the things that may cause you to fear. You were created for so much more than you can imagine. Do not let a fear of failure stop you from realizing your full potential.

ACCOUNTABILITY

When you add the often-overlooked element of accountability to establishing goals and action steps, the possibility of achieving meaningful goals increases exponentially. Accountability is essential to the process, but it is something with which most of us are uncomfortable. We are often more comfortable having others tell us what they think we want to hear, rather than telling the truth. The lack of accountability does not lead to change or growth—it leads to stagnation, ineffectiveness, and complacency. What if we embraced accountability? This is not a far-fetched notion. Many great leaders and performers have done just that.

Think of one of your sports heroes, a media star, or a leader in any field. What sets them apart from the average person? I would surmise that they have a strong vision of their desired future and they set meaningful goals. They also have a coach, mentor, or trusted partner who holds them accountable for practicing and taking the necessary steps to improve. Experiencing small measures of success creates the inspiration needed to stay true to the process and continue moving forward. When there is a setback, the coach or trusted partner provides the appropriate feedback.

We can all develop an appreciation for accountability. However, this will not happen overnight. In order for it to occur, we must be willing to be held accountable, and we must remain committed until we experience measures of success.

What step do you need to take today to begin the process of embracing accountability? It could be as simple as working with a coach, mentor, or trusted partner and giving them permission to hold you accountable. It could also be authentically connecting with direct reports and creating an environment in which others feel comfortable being honest with you and providing feedback. I encourage you to begin the process by taking a first step. Embracing accountability is possible, and it could lead to high levels of success and fulfillment for you and those with whom you collaborate.

Do you know of anyone who has accomplished something great without someone willing and available to hold them accountable? Although this does happen, it is more difficult to achieve your goals in such a situation. When I think of accountability, I think of having someone who has unbiased thoughts along with an understanding of what you are experiencing. They care, are willing to be honest, and wish to partner with you on the journey. They also demonstrate empathy and have your best interest at heart.

As a basketball player in high school and college, I realized the importance of having coaches who provided candid feedback and placed me in environments where I felt stretched. The coaches I had were experts at the game of basketball, and they knew how to maximize their players' efforts and potential. Some were low key and relaxed, while others were bold and assertive. They all provided feedback, and they encouraged me to practice until I got it right. I did not know it at the time, but the skills that I was learning were life skills, not just skills related to the basketball court. In addition to the coach, we players were quick to encourage and hold each other accountable. As a freshman in college, I landed a starting position on the team, which was very exciting for me. We had a point guard who was an upperclassman, a wizard with the basketball and, overall, a great guy. I remember him making encouraging comments about my potential as a young player. He felt that I had the ability to be a star. He challenged me in practice and on the court. It was a pleasure to play with James "Slick" Allen.

I also remember being part of an accountability group for men. We met early every Friday morning for an hour or two during a period in my life when I really needed this type of community. We were in similar life stages, with young families and demanding jobs. Needless to say, it was a stressful time in all of our lives. Prior to joining the group, I typically relied on myself to get things done. I did not trust others, and I was not very transparent nor vulnerable. I played the corporate role, which was straight-faced and rock solid. This translated into other areas of my life in an unconscious way. The pressure associated with this was not something that I understood well. The accountability group allowed me to grow in relationships with other men in a non-competitive environment that was caring and encouraging. We also became transparent and brutally honest with each other as trust developed within the group. This group met for approximately four years and, during this time, we all experienced loss and challenges in our lives. I can honestly say that I grew immensely as a husband, father, employee, leader, and family member, and in many other ways. This was a situation in which accountability became very real to me.

As with other things in life, time often becomes a barrier when it comes to building accountability in one's life. For instance, as a financial planner, I have noticed that most people need some type of relationship with someone who can help them develop a financial strategy based on their goals. Unfortunately, the profession has not fulfilled this role very well due to the nature of the business. In many respects, it is volume- and revenue-based, which affects the time professionals take to build relationships with clients. I expect this to continue to evolve as the industry develops. If you do not have accountability in the important areas of life, it would be in your best interest to get it. Sometimes just biting the bullet and hiring a coach or someone to advise and/or teach you can be transformational. I have seen this as a coach and a financial planner. People accomplish goals and reach levels beyond what they could on their own, and you can certainly do the same. If you do not currently have accountability, invite it into your life. You will benefit and be the better for it.

CHAPTER 7

CELEBRATE SUCCESS

M ost leaders are overburdened with objectives that need to be achieved in a relatively short timeframe, and they have never-ending responsibilities. Their focus is often on accomplishing the goal of the moment, after which they are encouraged to move on to the next pressing goal. This leads to a culture of busyness as well as a reluctance to take time to reflect on and celebrate success. In my work with coaching clients, I am often met with silence when I ask: "How will you celebrate your success?" It is important to take time to recognize and enjoy our progress and accomplishments.

Celebration can be defined as the action of marking one's pleasure at an important event or occasion by engaging in enjoyable, typically social, activity. Taking the time to properly celebrate the achievement of a goal or an objective can be motivational and inspirational. It can also serve as an impetus for making progress toward the achievement of other goals. A celebration does not need to be anything grand. It can be as simple as sitting and quietly relishing the thought that you achieved something that was important to you. Going out for ice cream or a cup of coffee can also be ways of celebrating. In fact, the options for celebrating success are limitless. It is important that you determine the method of celebration that is most meaningful to you. If you lead a team, it is important that you collaborate with team members to do the same for them.

Carefully consider how you will celebrate success when you set goals and develop action steps for achieving them. Make this an essential component of the goal-setting process, as it will serve to inspire you and those around you to higher levels of performance and success.

This can be a very difficult area for me as an achiever and a person who likes to look beyond the horizon to my next goal. I am slowly realizing the importance of reflecting on and appreciating the accomplishment of goals, regardless of how large or small. The journey of setting goals and taking action to achieve them is often challenging, and it takes an investment of time. Properly celebrating success can give you the fuel you need to move toward larger and more challenging goals. The definition of success here is achieving a worthwhile goal. If you are a goal setter, you can probably empathize with me. I successfully passed the CERTIFIED FINANCIAL PLANNER™ or CFP® exam. If you have ever taken the exam, you know the level of difficulty and the sacrifices that are necessary to complete the process. I worked on this goal for over two years. This consisted of months of study and preparation, and included a tremendous amount of spaced repetition. The exam is six hours long, and it can and normally does cover everything related to financial planning. After passing it, my mind immediately jumped to the next thing, which was getting a Registered Life Planner or RLP® designation which I have since completed. Then, the COVID-19 pandemic hit and everything went on hold. As I write this, I still have not properly celebrated my achievement of passing the CFP® exam. Writing this chapter has challenged me to do so.

The special recognition of your achievement should also include time for giving thanks. You have been equipped with the talent, time, and resources to achieve a goal that is important to you. I have come to understand that there is a spiritual component to goal setting. The benefit we get is who and what we become on the journey toward achieving the goal. I became more knowledgeable about money, but I also became more resilient and determined. It also forced me to believe more in myself, and my abilities, which will benefit me as I move forward. It was a blessing to achieve this goal, and I now intend to use these skills to influence the lives of my clients and others in a profound way. Financial literacy is not typically an area of focus in our consumer-based society. Therefore, my expertise offers me an opportunity to be a blessing and help people who have a need. This is certainly something of which to be thankful and celebrate. Learn to celebrate success if you have not already done so. Life is more than work. We must learn to stop, reflect, be thankful, and celebrate.

CONCLUSION

———

You have finished this book. Congratulations! It has been my pleasure to share some of my life experiences with you along with what certain secrets, principles, or nuggets I have learned from points throughout my life. I have shared a portion of my journey as I developed leadership skills and found ways to influence others through opportunities to use my gifts, abilities, and talents. Throughout most of my journey, I did not realize I was being shaped and molded by my experiences, which is one of the reasons I refer to them as "secrets" in the title of this book. If you have never reflected deeply on your life's journey, I encourage you to do so. I am sure you will find some hidden experiences and lessons that influenced and shaped you as well.

My hope is that you have reached a point where you can begin the process of developing your own strategic approach to life. That means clarifying your purpose and developing a vision of your desired future. Get that picture in your mind and develop your mission statement, which will probably be based on your vision and purpose. Afterward, evaluate and clarify your life's priorities. You should also make it a point to prioritize your priorities, assess how you are currently doing in each area of life, and determine your goals. Remember, goal setting is a key part of the process. After you have written your goals, develop action steps for each goal and place them in your calendar. It is helpful to track your activity, and account-ability is important as well. I have learned over the years that if you can believe in a goal, you can achieve it. In addition, do not forget about affirmations and visualization and the importance of celebrating your achievements.

Organizations view strategic planning as a vital element of their success. The focus of this book is on incorporating this concept into your life. There is no better time to take on this challenge and to help others do the same. I encourage you to continue to lead the field—whatever field in which you find yourself—and be a positive influence. My hope is that you will make it part of your mission to lead yourself well and find ways to positively influence and impact the lives of others. As we conclude, please know that you matter and the world really needs you and your gifts. So, LEADERFLUENCE! Be a gift to the world!

ABOUT THE AUTHOR

Mike Kelly is a coach, speaker, consultant, financial planner, author, and entrepreneur. He is a certified coach and a CER-TIFIED FINANCIAL PLANNER™, who is co-owner of Right Path Enterprises with his wife, Melinda, and Founder and Principal Advisor of Kelly Financial Planning. Prior to starting his businesses, Mike was an executive and senior leader with Michelin, Inc. and Macy's, Inc. He gained a broad base of experience in areas such as operations, human resources, finance, marketing, and sales. Mike was named *Alumnus of the Year* by his alma mater, Mars Hill University, and he currently serves as Chairman of the University's Board of Trustees in addition to serving and having served as a board member for a number of other organizations. He is a member of Rotary International and served as District Governor for the organization's Southwest Ohio Region during the 2016-2017 Rotary year. Mike has received a number of awards and recognition for his impact on the community and organizations over the years. He enjoys partnering with individuals and organizations to support them in achieving their goals and dreams. Mike holds a bachelor's degree from Mars Hill University and a master's degree in business administration from Webster University, where he was named Most Outstanding Graduate Student. He and Melinda reside in Cincinnati, Ohio. Connect with him at www. rightpathenterprises.com and www.kellyfinancialplanning. com

ACKNOWLEDGMENTS

First and foremost, I thank God for equipping me and for providing me with the opportunity to share my thoughts with you. I am indebted to my parents, Theodore and Lucille Kelly, for birthing me and providing a foundation that allowed me to grow into the person I am today.

I extend my heartfelt thanks to my beloved wife, Melinda, for encouraging me over the years to take the step of writing this book. Thank you to my son, Michael, for providing your input and support as I began the process and considered the relevance of my writing for the emerging generations.

I am thankful for and appreciate the support of my sister, Delores, and brothers, Willie James and Mickey, for your love and encouragement over the years. Thank you, too, to my extended family, especially my aunt, Dorothy Hughes.

I am also thankful to everyone who has been a part of this

process and all of you who have been, and continue to be, a part of my journey and to those of you who have allowed me the privilege of being part of yours.

IF YOU'RE A FAN OF THIS BOOK, WILL YOU HELP ME SPREAD THE WORD?

There are several ways you can help me get the word out about the message of this book…

- Post a 5-Star review on Amazon.
- Write about the book on your Facebook, Twitter, Instagram, LinkedIn—any social media you regularly use!
- If you blog, consider referencing the book, or publishing an excerpt from the book with a link back to my website. You have my permission to do this as long as you provide proper credit and backlinks.
- Recommend the book to friends—word-of-mouth is still the most effective form of advertising.
- Purchase additional copies to give away as gifts.

The best way to connect with me is by visiting
www.rightpathenterprises.com or **www.kellyfinancialplanning.com**.

NEED A DYNAMIC SPEAKER FOR YOUR NEXT EVENT?

How about coaching your group to the next level of success?

The best way to connect with me is by visiting
www.rightpathenterprises.com
or
www.kellyfinancialplanning.com.